REALITY, TRUTH AND EVIL

Facts, questions and perspectives on September 11, 2001

T.H. MEYER

With a timeline for 9.11.2001
by José García Morales

TEMPLE LODGE

Translated from German by Matthew Barton

Temple Lodge Publishing
Hillside House, The Square
Forest Row, RH18 5ES

www.templelodge.com

Published by Temple Lodge 2005

Originally published in German under the title *Der 11. September, das Böse und die Wahrheit, Fakten, Fragen, Perspektiven* by Perseus Verlag, Basel, Switzerland in 2004

A catalogue record for this book is available from the British Library

ISBN 1 902636 66 X

Cover montage of Pearl Harbor 1941 and New York 2001 by Rudolf Zimmermann
Cover layout by Andrew Morgan
Typeset by DP Photosetting, Aylesbury, Bucks.
Printed and bound by Cromwell Press Limited, Trowbridge, Wilts.

Contents

Preface

The tragic events of September 11 have triggered off a new era of international relations and politics: an era in which the supremacy and global leadership of the USA is spoken in an open fashion. The attacks were sudden and a surprise to the whole world, and yet, up to the present day, little in the way of real official investigation has occurred. The 9/11 Commission Report does not include crucial facts and is totally based on the 'surprise attack' theory.* Unofficial investigations by independent researchers, on the other hand, have shed significant light on the real character of those events. In the English-speaking world there are, among others, publications by Gore Vidal, Nafeez Ahmed and Michel Chossudovsky that study various aspects of the catastrophe. Last year, David Ray Griffin published *The New Pearl Harbor*, which has become something of a bestseller. Also, after many years in preparation, Michael Ruppert brought out his book *Crossing the Rubicon* in which he analyses the US military flight exercises that took place on September 11 and absorbed large parts of the US air defence capacity. These exercises, suggests Ruppert, led to confusion as to whether

---

* For a full discussion see David Ray Griffin's *The 9/11 Commission Report, Omissions and Distortions* (Arris Books 2004).

the real attacks were part of the exercise or not.

The essays in this book are not intended to add to the mass of independent investigations detailed in the above books and elsewhere, although some facts are referred to which have not been discussed previously. Rather, the approach of the essays is, on the whole, a symptomatic one. In other words, the present author has selected a few facts and events connected to 9/11 that seem to have far deeper implications than many other facts and data surrounding that day. A significant fact of this type is, for example, that on the very day of the attacks on New York and the Pentagon, the events were compared with the Japanese attack on Pearl Harbor in December 1941 which brought the United States into the Second World War. This comparison was not made by onlookers or commentators, but by the President of the United States and government insiders like Zbigniew Brzezinski. It was immediately taken up by the American and international media, and became the basis for the work of the US Commission which was to investigate the attacks.

As perfect as the analogy between Pearl Harbor and 9/11 may seem at first hand—both were allegedly 'surprise attacks'—a close study of both attacks (with the help of excellent existing investigations on Pearl Harbor) reveals that they were a surprise only for the mass population. However, in both cases, in 1941 as well as in 2001, certain individuals within the US administrations were well informed. Thus a closer look at Pearl Harbor—not undertaken from this specific point of view in the book by David Ray Griffin—is utilized as a starting point for a realistic understanding of the basic character of the events of September 11. Because of the central role of this comparison, a few repetitions in the various chapters were unavoidable—though they occur in somewhat different contexts.

The initial comparison is shown to be a deliberate application of a well-established popular myth, calculated to sway public opinion in the aftermath of the attacks into believing that there was, and still is, an all powerful external enemy. The whole world must fear this enemy—namely Islamic Terrorism—and unite, under the leadership of the United States of America, in hunting down and vanquishing it.

Some essays therefore explore the implications of deceiving people by the deliberate use of lies. Some aspects of the reality of destructive forces are investigated, and suggestions are made as to how such forces may be identified and dealt with. A further theme is the way in which conflicts of any kind, between religions, nations or individuals, are used to further particular policy objectives. Finally, there is a discussion of various ways of overcoming conflict through the harnessing of its inherent energy, i.e. using this energy for the resolution of conflict, as well as for greater social and spiritual development.

Rudolf Steiner pointed out on several occasions that the confrontation with, and the understanding of, destruction and evil is a task to be tackled by humanity for many centuries to come. He made clear that the primary instruments necessary for success in this task are clear observation and unbiased thinking. He also spoke of a growing tendency to undermine human beings' ability to think, a tendency which, he contends, manifests particularly markedly in western politics and the spiritual sources that stand behind it.

The attacks of 9/11 have brought to the surface a hitherto unknown quality of evil. Surrounded as these events are by myth and outright untruth, their aftermath, in terms of their official discussion and interpretation, exhibits a clear tendency towards a suppression of free thought. In this respect, too—and not only in the context of US geopolitics—they are truly significant and symptomatic.

The essays in this book thus also attempt to elaborate and discuss some of the deeper implications of this key event of our times.

Thomas H. Meyer
1 March 2005

Introduction

Unanswered questions

This book contains a number of observations about the crimes committed on September 11, 2001. So far these crimes have not been cleared up by the US administration in a full or transparent way. The administration and those sections of the national and international media which—for whatever reason—are more or less subservient to it, have largely restricted themselves to the endlessly repeated account of the official 'conspiracy theory'. The attacks on the World Trade Center, in this account, were firstly a *surprise* to everyone, and secondly were attributable to the activities of Islamic terrorists, whose active core is called 'al Qaeda'. This conspiracy theory has in the meantime been shaken, or even wholly refuted, by a series of independent investigations.

In the place of the discredited official conspiracy theory, questions remain which are still unanswered to this day:

- Where are the original passenger lists of the missing passengers and 'hijackers'?
- Where is the identification evidence for the (supposed) passengers on the four domestic flights?
- Where are the four black boxes belonging to the four aircraft?

- Where are the flight security recordings for the four flight routes?
- What do the confiscated surveillance camera video-tapes from the Pentagon and the Sheraton Hotel opposite it reveal?
- Etc. etc.

Gerhard Wisnewski has summarized these and other questions and inconsistencies in his new book.[1] The timeline by José García Morales on p. 111ff. of this book draws attention to further striking inconsistencies,

The following observations neither intend nor are able to give an exhaustive answer to such unresolved questions. They initially highlight phenomena which came to light long before September 11, creating an atmosphere of acquiescence towards official statements about the attacks: above all, for instance, a leader article with a map of the world from the financial magazine *The Economist,* as well as the ideas—some well known, others less so—of Samuel Huntington and Zbigniev Brzezinski (see p. 21f.).

We will also take a closer look at George W. Bush's sudden, bizarre interest in children at the time the catastrophe occurred (p. 29f.).

Pearl Harbor as the key to the September 11 attacks
Very special consideration, furthermore, is given to the comparison with Pearl Harbor which the President and other figures close to the administration trumpeted with apocalyptic pathos to the world, *on the very day of the*

attacks. The Japanese attack on the early morning of 7 December 1941 was cited in the mass media as the great precedent in American and even world history. But the myth of the malicious Japanese 'surprise attack' has long been refuted, with detailed revelations of the true nature of the attacks and the events surrounding them. Nevertheless, the administration relied on the Pearl Harbor *myth* having meanwhile become so firmly lodged in people's minds that it could base the first statements about September 11 being a 'surprise' attack on the Pearl Harbor events. In doing so, from the very first day of its 'investigations', it made a mockery not only of truth but also, in retrospect, of the 2,500 or so victims[2] of each catastrophe.

An analysis of this comparison (p. 37ff.) undertaken back in October 2001, and first published the following month in the *Europäer* magazine, revealed its simultaneously deceitful and cynical character. Deceitful in so far as it brought the Pearl Harbor *myth* back into emotional play, whipping up all America and a good deal of the rest of the world into remote-controlled indignation; and cynical in respect of those who know the *truth* about Pearl Harbor (Americans among them!). All that mattered was that the myth should be effective amongst the populace, who had been reminded of it only a few months before the attacks by a sentimental Hollywood film. But to those in the know (i.e. those who had proper information about the facts), this official comparison actually *provided the real key to understanding the attacks of 2001.* Those who use this key can regard the Pearl Harbor comparison as the point of departure for a critical assessment of all subsequent official statements about September 11. In relation to the work of the official investigative commission, for example, they will see how the Pearl Harbor *myth* played a fundamental role from the very beginning (see p. 68). They will also see that admissions regarding the 'failure' of security services have drawn on those which the Roberts Commission, the official investigative commission on Pearl Harbor, tried to assert. (In view of the similar 'failure' on September 11, which was the subject of immediate investigations and subsequent admissions, the well-documented and jolly party which George W. Bush held with George Tenet and his staff at CIA headquarters only two weeks after the attacks strikes one as very odd. Strangely, the critical literature on the attacks has, to my knowledge, completely overlooked or ignored this event; see pp. 24f. and 55f.)

Given all the subsequent inconsistencies or untruths in the official version of events, the manner in which the administration itself (and not just a few 'conspiracy theorists') brought Pearl Harbor into play as an historical parallel, can be regarded as a piece of brazen deception which sheds light on all subsequent official explanations about September 11.

The official investigative commission's concluding report—an establishment farce

On 22 July the 567-page concluding report by the official US investigative commission was published.[3] The concluding report consolidates the basic premise of all 'investigations' it describes: that this was a surprise attack planned and undertaken by al Qaeda. At the first public hearing on 31 March 2003, commission member Timothy Roemer cited the theses of Roberta Wohlstetter's 'outstanding' book, *Pearl Harbor, Warning and Decision,* to which Donald Rumsfeld had given eager publicity even before taking office (see p. 68). Roemer quoted the following words from the foreword:

> It was just a dramatic failure of a remarkably well-informed government to call the next enemy move in a Cold War crisis.

And he immediately applied this to the September 11 attacks:

> Today it might be some of the same words. It wasn't a Cold War crisis and it wasn't the Japanese, but it was al Qaeda.[4]

Besides Roemer, commission chairman Thomas Kean and commission member Richard Ben-Veniste also drew on this deceptive comparison with Pearl Harbor.

Kean, who was appointed by Bush, had nevertheless warned from the outset against expecting too much of the results of the investigation. He saw the September 11 commission as a successor to the Roberts and Warren commissions, whose stated aim was to clear up the events of Pearl Harbor and the murder of JFK. Kean had already washed his hands in advance when he stated that none of them fulfilled the hopes invested in them.[5] Why such a grave reservation before the enquiry had even begun?

In section 11 of the concluding report ('Hindsight and Foresight'), the aim, as one might have predicted, is to finally set in stone the arbitrary thesis underpinning the commission's work. For this purpose it once again resorts to Wohlstetter's authority—in her words:

> [It is] much easier after the event to sort the relevant from the irrelevant signals. After the event, of course, a signal is always crystal clear; we can now see what disaster it was signaling since the disaster has occurred. But before the event it is obscure and pregnant with conflicting meanings.[6]

Thus the report concludes by once again casting the many-layered crime of September 11, 2001 in the false light of the earlier 'surprise attack'.

Meanwhile, however, independent researchers have undertaken meticulous investigation that is available on the internet and at unofficial 9/11 conferences; and at the same time a general awareness has grown about the true nature of the 'surprise attack' on Pearl Harbor, not least thanks to the book *Day of Deceit* by Robert Stinnett published in 2000 (see pp. 39f.). Commission members loyal to the administration may have grown more cautious in relation to this theme. Kean, for instance, when presenting the report on 22 July 2004 to a crowd of journalists in Washington, said: 'Some of us compared the shock we felt to Pearl Harbor, others to the Kennedy assassination. *There is no comparison.* This was a moment unique [...] in our long history.'[7] It now seems that those who drew on this comparison are gradually coming to be wary of it, as more and more people start to interpret it in a quite different way than Wohlstetter, Rumsfeld, Bush & Co. intended. With good reason: Pearl Harbor *is* in many respects a true forerunner and precedent for September 11, 2001.

Of the carefully chosen troupe of journalists to whom the report (shortly after its release on the internet) was first presented by the commission of ten, only one raised a critical question: Why was there no enquiry into the business links between the Bush family and the bin Laden family, which Michael Moore also highlighted in his film *Fahrenheit 9/11?* Kean replied that he hadn't seen 'Mr Moore's film', and was thus unaware of his precise accusations.

Of the many essential facts not even touched on in the report, I will focus on just a single one. On 9 October 2002 on PBS, a private TV company, Larry Silverstein, leaseholder of the two WTC towers, stated that building no. 7 which collapsed at 5.20 pm despite the fact that no aeroplane had hit it and only a small fire had broken out inside it, had been 'pulled' (i.e. demolished). The decision to 'pull it' down was made together with the chief of the fire services. Silverstein said: 'I remember getting a call from the fire department commander, telling me that they were not sure they were gonna be able to contain the fire, and I said, "We've had such terrible loss of life, maybe the smartest thing to do is pull it." And they made that decision to pull and we watched the building collapse.'[8]

The two towers also collapsed into themselves in a similar fashion and were literally pulverized, indicating a professionally organized controlled explosion.

The report refrains from specifically attributing blame and, in accordance with its predetermined and inexorable direction, it blames everything on a complex set of individual errors and deficient cooperation between the CIA, FBI and the US administration.

Recommendations for the future are, in contrast, not lacking.

An anti-terror Tsar (sic!) is to be appointed to coordinate the work of all secret services. His budget will ensure that the CIA and other services can 'employ the right people' (Kean).

Of special importance is the fact that both Thomas Kean and Lee Hamilton told journalists on several occasions that another, similar attack would occur. And since, in contrast to former assertions, it was admitted that al Qaeda has no links with Iraq but, as now claimed, probably with *Iran,* one can fear the worst.

The true function of the official concluding report is thus to finally drum into the skulls of people both in the US and the whole world *the myths of the surprise attack and the decisive involvement of al Qaeda,* and, still more importantly perhaps, *to spread expectation of future attacks,* which the administration must confront with increased expenditure and more stringent measures.

No wonder that, in a carefully stage-managed performance on the White House lawn, George W. Bush accepted the report from the hands of Kean and Lee Hamilton (commission vice-president) with full satisfaction, thanking the commission for its good work and 'very constructive recommendations'.

On 22 July 2004, speaking to the BBC's World Service, former CIA analyst Ray McGovern said the fact that no single person had been called to account was an insult to the victims of the attack, and went on to suggest the investigation was a whitewash: 'This is an establishment report, much in the vein of Butler and Hutton.' One hand washes the other.

As far as truth is concerned, the US report was already so much waste paper before a single line of it had been published.

As symptom of the likelihood of still worse developments to come in the USA, however, it should be taken very seriously.

The need for broad perspectives
September 11, 2001 is an event of global dimensions, comparable to 28 June 1914. As we know, the attack on that date led to one of the defining catastrophes of the 20th century. Similarly, September 11 has unleashed a fundamental catastrophe of the 21st century, which has now been raging for three years.

An analysis, indeed a meticulously truthful anatomy of this event, is thus as essential here as for the start of the First World War. To undertake this, two things seem to me to be necessary:

Firstly, much detailed research needs to be done to resolve the open questions formulated by Gerhard Wisnewski and others, or to highlight who is rendering their solution difficult or even impossible, and by what means.

Secondly—to avoid losing one's way in the thicket of detailed questions—each set of conclusions needs to be repeatedly illumined from broad perspectives, as can be done for instance by drawing on the philosophy of G.W.F. Hegel, or the spiritual science of Rudolf Steiner (see p. 91). Such perspectives include the following:[9]

- All natural development in the world occurs via alternating polar processes and their synthesis (connection). One need only think of the contrasting opposites of day and night, cold and heat, life and death; then of the contrasts between the sexes, the various human races, peoples, nations or 'civilizations'. In the field of human knowledge, one can apply this first and foremost to the contrast between perception and concept, and then to that between deception and reality.
- As human beings we can rediscover these contrasts as the foundation of our own development. Our task is not *to create new opposites* or conflicts, but *to overcome those already present,* above all those of a sexual, national, religious, cultural or epistemological nature.[10] Those who strive for this kind of higher

unity between opposites are advancing human development. Those, on the other hand, who try to fix and perpetuate such contrasts, or even to create new ones artificially, oppose this development.

Such perspectives give us a standard to help distinguish between strivings truly worthy of human beings and those which only serve certain individual or group egotisms. To the latter type belong the Nazi and Bolshevik systems, but also, and no less so, the Anglo-American system which not only helped cultivate the former but has also survived them, and is now becoming a threat to the whole planet.

A look at 'Skull & Bones'
Certain Anglo-American societies such as the Yale club 'Skull & Bones' that has been in the news recently can best be characterized by their intention to use existing conflicts or create new ones—as Anthony Sutton described over 20 years ago. At the same time these efforts often give the appearance of intending to broker deals and resolve disputes, whereas in reality they exacerbate and exploit them for maximum advantage.

One need only cast a glance on peace negotiations aided by British and American diplomacy over the last hundred years. Why did almost all of them fail? Because in reality the aim was to gain *power* through exploiting (and increasing) conflict. The enormous increase in US power in recent years is also based on the exploitation of conflicts which are first exacerbated if not wholly created. First the spectre of a 'clash of civilizations' and of an 'Islamic world' which threatens 'western values' is disseminated across the globe. Then, following attacks by 'Islamic terrorists', one can advance to a *harvest of power,* from Afghanistan through Iraq to Palestine.

Whether or not increasing numbers of people can acquire a clear understanding of the two ways of handling conflicts will be decisive for the further course of the 21st century.

Anyone who believes that a 'war on terror' has been going on since September 11, 2001 is deceived by appearances. In reality what is at stake is the consolidation and globalization of the USA's dominance, the 'sole truly global superpower' (Brzezinski). In this battle waged particularly with financial means (finance and raw materials markets) by a British-American elite, US Presidents and their administrations only act as marionettes and play walk-on parts. How little is dependent at a certain level on the much-vaunted 'contrasts' between Presidents is clear from the simple fact that both the current US President and his challenger in the last election, Kerry, belong to the same Skull & Bones club. It is part of the technique of power to conjure up the appearance of conflict and difference where these do not in fact exist.

After so much 'successful' deception in the 20th century, we can assume that the groups striving for power will attempt to bring the 'deception principle' to bear in a still more radical way than hitherto.

Prohibition on thinking, or independent judgements?

This also includes efforts to control human thinking on a global scale. One can observe this particularly clearly in the debate about September 11, 2001. The most dire means so far used against all those who question the official version of events is the attempt to set critics of the September 11 myth on a par with Holocaust deniers. This happened for instance in a series of *Arte* TV programmes on 13 April 2004, which drew on the unspeakable *Spiegel* articles of 8 September and 27 October 2003 and went one step further in promoting their defamatory character. One broadcast that evening was entitled 'September 11 did not take place'. To properly assess the comparison suggested by this title, one has to remember that the—naturally absurd—denial of the Holocaust is a *punishable crime* in Germany.

Gerhard Wisnewski comments on this: 'If this parallel between 9/11 sceptics and Holocaust deniers succeeds, efforts could be made over a longer or shorter period to prohibit all critical statements about the attacks on 9/11. It would naturally be still better to equate Holocaust deniers with conspiracy theorists, for this would mean that, in future, public comments about the background to any event could be outlawed.'[11] Wisnewski speaks in this context of a 'prohibition on thinking'.

The onset of such a danger was urgently stressed almost 90 years ago, in the middle of the First World War:

> Shortly after the year 2000 a kind of indirect prohi-
> bition on thinking will emanate from America, a law
> which will aim to suppress all individual thought.[12]

This sentence was uttered by the philosopher and
founder of spiritual science Rudolf Steiner, in a lecture
he gave on 4 April 1916.

The same Steiner was also of the deeply-held convic-
tion that our era faces all human beings with the task of
confronting the powers of evil by all available instruments of knowledge—above all by acquiring an
unwavering discernment for truth and deception.[13] It is
this capacity of discernment which the 'prohibition on
thinking' aims to deaden or even destroy.

A very direct means of implementing this prohibition
is to *intentionally* spread untruth and lies. This disables
human beings' capacity to distinguish what is true and
what is not. This 'technique of evil' which certain groups
used consciously in relation to information about the
events of September 11, is something which Steiner also
commented on in a very far-sighted way:

> Those who are expert at such things, what do they do?
> If one is expert in this then one uses one's authority to
> tell people things that are untrue. One does this sys-
> tematically. By doing so one dulls their awareness to
> the level of hazy, dream consciousness. One thereby
> undermines the individual consciousness that has
> been developing in human souls since the 15th century
> [. . .] One tries to deaden awareness by teaching people
> lies. We naturally have to fight lies and untruth with

all the means at our disposal. But one should not believe that they arise from simple misconception or the belief that what is said is true.[14]

Clarification and refutation of the myths surrounding September 11, which independent researchers of all nationalities have undertaken with the means available to them, is thus not least a sorely needed battle very much in keeping with our times to maintain and further develop our *individual human power of judgement and discernment*. It is to this battle against a global deadening of human awareness that the present collection of reflections aims to contribute.

1

'Islamistan' and the West

The consensus on the new world order—before and after September 11, 2001

£210,423

Proclamation of the new world order by Bush senior on 11 September 1990

On 11 September 1990, before both houses of Congress, President Bush senior spoke for the first time of the need to establish a 'new world order'. This was after the Iraqi army invaded Kuwait. This 'new era', he promised, would be 'freer from the threat of terror, stronger in the pursuit of justice, and more secure in the quest for peace.'[1]

In the week prior to this, a 'new and accurat map of the world' [sic] appeared in the London *Economist,* proposing a new division of the world's continents according to religious and philosophical perspectives.

On this much-debated map, Europe is, on the one hand, absorbed into the West ('Euro-America'), and on the other merged with the East ('Euro-Asia'). Apart from this we find wholly new 'religious' continents: 'Islamistan', 'Hindustan' and 'Confuciania'. This map's cultural or religious continents are in the process of gradual realization. Throughout the world, for instance, one can clearly discern the establishment of an Islamic fundamentalist power block—Islamistan.

In the summer of 1993, in a widely acclaimed article in the *Foreign Affairs* journal, which has a major influence on US foreign policy, Samuel Huntington spoke of the new 'clash of civilizations'. At the same time he referred to the growing terrorist potential of Islamic fundamentalism, and soon afterwards this article was published in expanded book form.[2]

In 1997, in his book *The Grand Chessboard*, Zbigniew Brzezinski bluntly described the geostrategic and economic goals of US policy in Eurasia, characterizing the Islamic region of Afghanistan as a new Eurasian crisis area, while Europe, he suggested, should merely play the role of US vassal. According to Brzezinski, a general consensus for such a US policy would however be harder to establish than in 1941 (after the attack on Pearl Harbor), 'except in the circumstances of a truly massive and widely perceived direct external threat'.[3]

The effect of the September 11 attacks

On September 11, 2001, this 'external threat' became a globally perceived reality. But above and beyond the horror and mourning for innocent victims in New York (and subsequently in Afghanistan), we should not overlook the fact that this appalling event bore the following fruits as viewed from the perspective of the Brzezinski doctrine and Bush policies: 1) Announcements of solidarity with the US administration's future intentions by NATO heads of state immediately following September 11 have advanced the establishment of the 'Euro-American' block more than anything else. 2) More than any other event, September 11 massively consolidated establishment of the 'Islamistan' block.

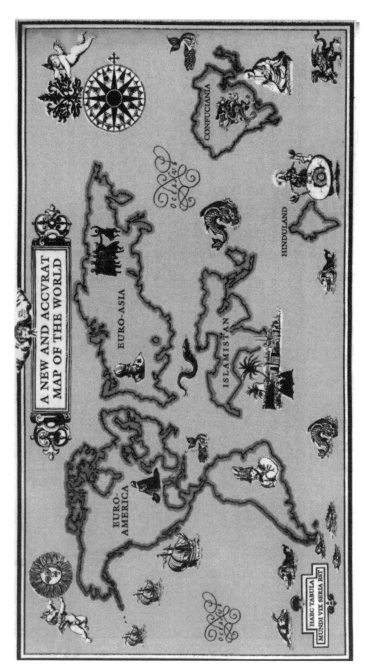

The 'new and accurat' map of the world published in September 1990 by The Economist

3) More than any other event, September 11 gave the US government dominance of its own jurisdiction over all national legislative structures. 4) More than any other event, September 11 gave the USA a free hand in the geopolitically important (i.e. drugs and oil trading) areas of the Near East (and no doubt soon also in Iraq and Saudi Arabia).

Celebrations at CIA headquarters

In view of this enormous 'usefulness' of the September 11 attacks for certain US circles, we have to ask to what extent this event can be explained solely in relation to Islamic fundamentalist groups, and how far it may in fact have been engineered in quite other, concealed ways.

The former German minister and secret service specialist Andreas von Bülow holds the view that both Huntington's and Brzezinski's publications may in some way have been unofficially commissioned by the CIA.[4] At CIA headquarters in Langley (Virginia), Bush junior celebrated a kind of promotional party just two weeks after the attacks, assuring the assembled CIA officials (including their boss George Tenet): 'September 11th is a sad memory, but it's a memory [...] And I can't thank you enough on behalf of the American people.'[5] This is not to claim that the CIA (or the FBI) *planned* the attacks themselves, but simply to ask: Did the US secret services *actively help* their successful execution? If the attacks were attributable solely to a purely passive 'failure' by the secret services, Bush junior would hardly have had grounds to celebrate at CIA headquarters on 26 September 2001.

Which conspiracy theory?

Conspiracy theories? This phrase is almost invariably used by those who have uncritically adopted the officially propounded *American* conspiracy theory. But this is the least convincing of all theories so far proposed about a September 11 conspiracy. It is an almost wholly unproven assertion, focusing entirely on bin Laden; and those who promote it have so far undertaken no systematic investigations or comprehensive efforts at clarification of the numerous unresolved questions, let alone presented any serious results. Nor have they cleared up questions which may be rather more than secondary, such as: What was there to celebrate in Langley on 26 September? Or—to take just a single one of the host of questions: Why did General Ahmed, the Pakistan intelligence services chief (who was in Washington at the time of the attacks and whose service—ISI—is known to work in the closest cooperation with the CIA), transfer 100,000 dollars to the account of terrorist pilot Mohamed Atta in the weeks before the attacks?[6]

A new world order for all

Brzezinski knew in 1997 that without 'a truly massive and widely perceived direct external threat' it would be difficult to gain a general consensus for the planned geostrategic policy of the new world order. *This consensus was established at one fell swoop by the events of*

September 11, 2001, in the interests of relatively few beneficiaries, and to the detriment of large portions of the world population (including the American people, on whom were clamped dictatorial 'homeland security' laws).

The world has not, as Bush senior's slogan-type proclamation stated on 11 September 1990, become 'freer from the threat of terror, stronger in the pursuit of justice, and more secure in the quest for peace'. And least of all through the policies of Bush junior's cabinet. It is surely time for a new world order that serves *all* of humanity.

2

The President who stayed in primary class

The video recordings of G.W. Bush at Booker School
The visit to Emma Booker School in Sarasota, Florida, by the President 'elected' through vote manipulation in Florida, was recorded on video.

For some time the Booker School had a link on its website to this video footage (running time: 11 minutes). Later it was removed.

At this point I will insert a quotation from Jared Israel (founder of the Emperor's Clothes website), one of the first American analysts of the inconsistencies in official statements about September 11. Jared Israel regards this video of Bush's visit to a school class as the first indication of criminal connivance or involvement by the US administration. The article (with links to the video) can be found at www.emperors-clothes.com/indict/vid.htm

Israel comments on the footage as follows:

This Short Clip is a Smoking Gun
In the short clip Bush is seen sitting in a classroom observing a reading lesson. Immediately Andrew Card, his Chief of Staff, hurries over and whispers something in his ear. Bush makes no reply. Andrew Card rushes off. What is wrong with this picture?

According to the official account, Andrew Card whis-

pered that a second plane had hit the World Trade Center and there was a national emergency.

Here's how Bush described that moment at a California Town Hall meeting, January 5th:
'*Andy Card came and said, "America is under attack." '*[1]

If his Chief of Staff tells the President the country is under attack, the President would discuss it. He would ask questions. Demand more information. Leave the room. Meet with advisers. Do something. But Bush just sat there.

The Chief of Staff is the President's employee. If he tells the President, 'America is under attack' the President would give him orders. But Bush said nothing—not one word. And Andy Card didn't wait for instructions; he rushed away.

What does this mean?

It means Andy Card did not expect a response.

It means he cannot have been informing Bush that an unexpected *national attack was underway.*

It means he was giving Bush an update on the progress of a plan of which Bush was already aware, and he had to get back to work.

And as for Bush, later in the short clip he is seen smiling and giving a pep talk to the children. In the full version, you can see him cheering the students and then giving them a longer pep talk when the lesson is over.

This is not the picture of a President stunned by an horrific event and confronted with an unexpected national emergency. This is the picture of treason.

Chief of Staff Card whispers to Bush in front of pupils at Emma Booker School: 'America is under attack'

II. Banter at Booker School

The original text on the Bush video clip soundtrack is reproduced below. Brief incomprehensible comments are indicated by [. . .].

[At around 8.47 am: first aeroplane strikes the WTC North Tower. Around 16 minutes later (9.03 am): second aeroplane strikes the South Tower. At shortly before nine, Bush arrives at the school with a police escort. He tells headteacher Rigell about the 'accident' with the first plane, stressing that the session at the school will take place as planned.[2]]

Bush: 'Good morning! Good morning!' [...] 'Great to meet everybody!' [To the children:] 'How are you doing? Are you OK?'
[Directly after Andy Card had supposedly informed Bush of the strike on the North Tower:]

Bush: 'Uh, these are great readers!'
Teacher: 'Yes, they are.'
Bush: 'Very impressive! Thank you all so very much for showing me your reading skills.'
[To the teacher:] 'I bet they practised it. [...]'
Teacher: 'Oh, yes, oh yes [...]'
Bush: 'Reading more than they watch TV?'
Teacher: 'Oh yes, oh yes.'
Bush [to the children:] 'Anybody do that? Read more than you watch TV?'
[Hands go up] 'Oh, that's great! Very good!'
'[...] Very important to practise. Thanks for having me. Very impressive!' [Shuts reader and stands up.]

[About 10 to 15 minutes later: first statement in front of gathered teachers, pupils and staff at Booker School.]

'Ladies and gentlemen, this is a difficult moment for America. I, em, unfortunately will be going back to Washington after my remarks. Secretary [...] will take the podium and discuss education. [...] I do want to thank you folks here at the [looks at the script in front of him] Booker Elementary School, for your hospitality. Today we've had a national tragedy. Two airplanes have

Three stills from the 11-minute Booker School video

crashed into the World Trade Center, in an apparent
terrorist attack on our country. I have spoken to the
Vice President, to the governor of New York, to the
director of the FBI, and I have ordered that the full
resources of the Federal Government go to help the
victims and their families, and to conduct a full-scale
investigation to hunt down and find those folks who
committed this act. Terrorism against our nation will
not stand. And now, if you join me in a moment of
silence. [The gathered school staff and Bush bow their
heads.] May God bless the victims, their families and
America. Thank you very much.' Takes sheets from the
lectern and goes. Bush leaves Booker School at 9.45 am.

3

The attacks on the World Trade Center—a multi-layered catastrophe

'Veritas magna est et praevalebit'[1]

1. The 'Pearl Harbor' effect

Almost all the media, particularly in the English-speaking world, drew a comparison with Pearl Harbor in the first days after the New York and Washington catastrophe.

It is well known that the supposedly surprise attack by Japanese military air power on the American Pacific base on 7 December 1941 brought the USA into the Second World War. Even though this comparison has taken a back seat in the intervening period, it gave rise to a major resurgence of American patriotism, one actually comparable to the patriotic war mood which took hold throughout America in response to what Roosevelt dramatically termed the 'Day of Infamy'.

Under the bold headline 'A cause for anger and retaliation', the special September issue of *Time* magazine carried the following appeal: 'What's needed is a unified, unifying sort of purple American fury—a

> **What's needed is a unified, unifying, Pearl Harbor sort of purple American fury – a ruthless indignation that doesn't leak away in a week or two**

ruthless   indignation that doesn't leak away in a week or two.'[2] On numerous occasions the position of Bush was compared with that of Roosevelt, who suc-cessfully used Japan's 'surprise attack' to lead a previously reluctant but now fully deter-mined American people into the Second World War, on the back of a massive change of mood. One can even say that this event gave him the moral permission to prosecute the war. Roosevelt led the Americans into the Second World War while Bush openly proclaimed the *first war of the 21st Century*, which it was America's task to fight and win. No peace-loving person, therefore, should lightly dismiss this parallel with the events of 1941, drawn immediately after the catastrophe. Nothing so effectively harnessed the emotions of hatred and revenge unleashed amongst large swathes of the American public by the events of September 11, and moulded them into a solid US patriotism, than did this new conjuring of a collective memory of what most Americans (and most educated Europeans) regard as the sole compar-able precedent in their history.

Thus the Pearl Harbor effect was immediately and

effectively linked with the reactions of horror to September 11, and not just by anyone but by Bush's government team. The comparison between the attacks on the World Trade Center and the Japanese attack on the American base was first voiced in the Air Force One aircraft in which the President flew to Nebraska on September 11.[3] It was immediately taken up by Republican Senator Hagel and Henry Kissinger.[4] The US geostrategist Brzezinski also stated in an interview on 13 September: 'This is without doubt the most murderous event experienced by the USA since the Civil War. It is more murderous even than Pearl Harbor, and the psychological impact is the same. In both cases a surprise attack was involved.'[5]

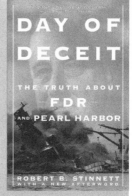

From the preface by Robert Stinnett to his book *Day of Deceit, The Truth About FDR and Pearl Harbor*[6]

This book contradicts and questions much of what has been written about the events and decisions that led to Japan's attack on Pearl Harbor on December 7, 1941. My sole purpose is to uncover the true story of events leading up to the devastating attack on the naval base and adjoining army facilities, and to document that it was not a surprise to President Franklin Delano Roosevelt and many of his top military and policy advisers...

As a veteran of the Pacific War I felt a sense of outrage

as I uncovered secrets that had been hidden from Americans for more than fifty years. But I understood the agonizing dilemma faced by President Roosevelt. He was forced to find circuitous means to persuade an isolationist America to join in a fight for freedom. He knew this would cost lives. How many, he could not have known.

The country was disillusioned by the failure of America's idealistic commitment to make 'the world safe for democracy' in World War I. Many Americans had chosen isolationism to shelter their young from the horrors of another war, and believed that Roosevelt would 'not send their sons to fight in foreign wars.' Roosevelt believed that his countrymen would rally to oppose an overt act of war on the United States. The decision he made, in concert with his advisors, was to provoke Japan through a series of actions into an overt act: the Pearl Harbor attack...

Eight steps were suggested to provoke a Japanese attack. Shortly after reviewing these, Roosevelt put them into effect. After the eighth provocation had been taken, Japan responded. On November 27 and 28, 1941, US military commanders were given this order: 'The United States desires that Japan commit the first overt act.' According to Secretary of War Henry L. Stimson, the order came directly from President Roosevelt.

[...] We have long known that Japanese diplomatic cables—which pointed towards hostilities—were intercepted and decoded. What I have discovered, however, is that we knew much more. Not only did we undertake provocative steps, we intercepted and decoded military cables. We knew the attack was coming.

By provoking the attack, Roosevelt accepted the terrible

truth that America's military forces—including the Pacific Fleet and the civilian population in the Pacific—would sit squarely in harm's way, exposed to enormous risks. The commanders in Hawaii, Admiral Husband Kimmel and Lieutenant General Walter Short, were deprived of intelligence that might have made them more alert to the risks entailed in Roosevelt's policy [...] More than 20,000 documents and interviews have led me to these conclusions. I am indebted to the Freedom of Information Act (FOIA) and its author, the late Congressman John Moss (D., CA) for making it possible for me to tell this story [...]

2. The truth about Pearl Harbor and some of its chief witnesses

Brzezinski's assertion about the 'surprise nature' of the Japanese attack is a prime example of the way this event is described in official US history, and is publicized to this day by 'court historians' and the 'court media' in America and the rest of the 'free world'. This is understandable, for it is only due to the first psychological Pearl Harbor effect of 1941 that it proved possible to involve the American people in the World War without resistance, urged on by moral indignation and noble duty. In view of such, for them, positive effects, those in power and their court historians have no interest in letting their version of events be replaced by another, even if it is true. That is why these court media do not as a rule take any notice of extensive Pearl Harbor research, right up to the present, by independent historians. It is understandable that truthful analysis of the facts by those whose research is in some way intertwined with power groups is only likely to the extent that such facts do not collide with the interests of those in power.

The latest independent research into Pearl Harbor was written by Robert B. Stinnett who served in the US navy between 1942 and 1946. He wrote a book about George Bush senior and worked as photographer and journalist for the *Oakland Tribune*. He advises the BBC and various Japanese TV stations as a specialist on the Pacific war.

Stinnett's book, entitled *Day of Deceit,* was published

Admiral Husband E. Kimmel

by Simon & Schuster in 2000. The title already hints at what really lay behind Roosevelt's 'Day of Infamy': a huge and yet largely successful manoeuvre of deceit against the country and Congress. Stinnett never questions the legitimacy of America entering the war, but just uncovers the impure means to this end, which led to the deaths of thousands of American citizens—2,476 American dead and 64 Japanese.

The main findings of his research, which took 17 years to complete, are clearly summarized by Stinnett in the preface to his book (see box pp. 39–41). Of particular interest here is the role of Roosevelt's war minister Henry L. Stimson—a member, by the way, of Yale's 'Skull & Bones' club—who, under a diary entry for 25 November 1941, reports a cabinet meeting which discussed ways of provoking the Japanese to strike first. Stimson stated: 'The question was how we should maneuver them into the position of firing the first shot without allowing too much danger to ourselves.' (See Charles A. Beard, *President Roosevelt and the Coming of the War 1941*, New Haven 1948, p. 516.) Stinnett also draws attention to the fact that certain intercepted Japanese messages dating back to the autumn of 1941 are still being withheld from the public.

The earliest, full-scale independent investigation into Pearl Harbor is probably that by the American academic historian George Morgenstern (1906-1988), entitled *Pearl Harbor, The Story of the Secret War,* and published in 1947 by a small New York publishing house (Devin Adair Company). Morgenstern comes to

Pearl Harbor on 7 December 1941

more or less the same conclusions as Stinnett, despite having access to far fewer records and documents.

Between Morgenstern's book and that by Stinnett come other works which focus more or less centrally on Pearl Harbor, by Charles Tansill (1890–1964), Harry Elmer Barnes (1889–1968), and Hamilton Fish (1888–1991). Tansill was one of the best-known US historians and held a chair at Georgetown University. For ten years he worked as adviser to the Senate Committee on Foreign Relations. His book, *Back Door to War*, was published in 1952. Barnes, one of the most important US historians of his generation, compiled his research on Pearl Harbor shortly before his death, under the title

Pearl Harbor After a Quarter of a Century (New York 1972). Hamilton Fish published his book *The Other Side of the Coin, How We Were Tricked Into World War II* (Vantage Press, New York) in 1976.

Of great significance is the statement quoted by Walter Post in the introduction to the German edition of Morgenstern's book,[7] by former CIA chief William Casey (who, among other things, played a major role in building up the Mujahidin in Afghanistan in the 80s). This is contained in his posthumous memoirs (see box, p. 50).

Similarly important material collected by Morgenstern and Stinnett was also compiled in a BBC film, 'Sacrifice at Pearl Harbor', written and produced by Roy Davies (in the series 'Our Century'; cablecast December 1989, on the Arts & Entertainment Network).

In May 2001, the magazine *GEO* published a thoroughly researched Pearl Harbor article by Wolf Schneider, entitled 'Pearl Harbor—Angriff im Morgengrauen' ('Pearl Harbour—attack at first light'). In this, Schneider quotes war minister Stimson's diary entry after receiving the 'terrible news'. Stimson stated that his first feeling was one of relief that the indecision was now over and that they were now in a crisis situation which would unite the whole country. In relation to the first cabinet meeting after the attack became known, Roosevelt's adviser Harry Hopkins reported that there wasn't an especially tense atmosphere. Labor minister Frances Perkins got a 'sneaky' sense from the President. The main theme of the meeting was how the President would explain to Congress, the country and the world what should now happen after this debacle.

Schneider also cites a notable comment by the Kennedy and Johnson adviser McGeorge Bundy—also a Skull & Bones member like Stimson and the three Bush generations. Looking back on the Pearl Harbor catastrophe Bundy says that it was a 'dreadful day but had a really wonderful result'. He adds that if some Americans think one shouldn't have had to pay the bloody price of 7 December, they ought to remember that 30 people died at Hiroshima for each one killed at Pearl Harbor.

At this point I want to bring in the American writer Gore Vidal, whose father was air travel minister under Roosevelt, and whose half-sister was Jacqueline Bouvier-Kennedy. 'No one is a better scourge of American foreign policy than he, and no one better knows the secrets of power,' wrote Willi Winkler in *Weltwoche* on 23 September 2001. And in connection with Vidal's latest novel *The Golden Age,* he writes:

> On Tuesday of last week the whole world was appalled. Sixty years after the attack on Pearl Harbor America was once again under attack and, as before, the 'Day of Infamy' slogan was going the rounds. US President Franklin Roosevelt coined this phrase, for the Japanese had allegedly given no warning before attacking on Sunday morning, 7 December 1941. On the following day the USA declared war on Japan, and Japan's ally Germany declared war on the USA three days later—turning

a European war into a world war. The sad story has only just been retold, in particularly bittersweet fashion, in the newly released film *Pearl Harbor*. And why did these things not actually happen the way they are portrayed in the cinema, embellished by a moving love story? Because the story simply isn't true. Who says so? Gore Vidal.[8]

From the new foreword to the German edition of:

Pearl Harbor, The Story of the Secret War
By George Morgenstern

Contrary to statements by the Roosevelt Administration, the Japanese command had, in the months before Pearl Harbor, tried desperately to reach a peaceful settlement of the disputes between America and Japan. When Roosevelt initiated a trade war against Japan, in particular an oil embargo, the Japanese leadership was left only with the choice of either submitting to unacceptable American demands, or taking forcible control of the raw material-rich areas of South-East Asia, above all the oil fields of the Dutch East Indies. Only when there was really no further prospect of a diplomatic solution did Tokyo finally decide to wage war. This decision came at the end of November 1941.

For their transatlantic telephone conversations, Churchill and Roosevelt used a so-called scrambling telephone which made the words spoken unintelligible unless one had a piece of de-scrambling equipment. By the end of 1940 the German Reichspost had succeeded in developing this equipment. In the summer of 1941 the Reichspost set up a surveillance station on the Dutch coast to listen in to transatlantic telephone calls, and from 11 September began to record them. On 26 November 1941 the German monitoring station took down a conversation between Churchill and Roosevelt in which the British Premier urgently warned the American President about a Japanese fighter carrier group that had just set off from a secret marine base in the north of Japan and was heading for Pearl Harbor.

Of course, one has to question the authenticity of a document containing such explosive revelations. There are strong indications that it is genuine. For one thing, General Marshall stated at a Joint Committee hearing that the American government had known the Germans were tapping the telephone conversations between Churchill and Roosevelt. For another, the former CIA chief William Casey wrote in his memoirs that the British had warned Washington of a Japanese fighter group that was heading towards Hawaii. [See p. 50.]

3. Giving untruth the stamp of truth

The weight of evidence which investigations since the 40s of the last century have brought to light is so conclusive that the official version of the 'surprise attack' on Pearl Harbor represents a brazen farce for those with a sense of reality about these matters. Roosevelt's policies required a *lie* in order to make headway, just as an ordinary engine needs oil to function. So can it be regarded as an exception in American and—if one considers the Hitler regime which ran exactly parallel to Roosevelt's government—European politics of the 20th century?

What is certain is that the objective untruth about Pearl Harbor has succeeded in anchoring itself as a great and tragic historical truth amongst broad swathes of the population. And furthermore, this great historical truth was the very first 'truth' to be associated with an apparently similar catastrophe—that of September 11, 2001. In assessing the real facts, is it not quite justified for every person who knows the truth about Pearl Harbor to ask whether, in explanations given about the background to September 11, nothing but truth has followed *that great initial lie?*

Why do we attribute such significance to these things?

Because untrue, false ideas themselves act as destructive powers. And those who view *this* kind of destructive power as minor, or even non-existent in comparison with the destruction of skyscrapers and human lives, show only that they possess no sense of the reality of the human soul and spirit, regarding the destruction of life and architectural complexes as the only real and serious kind of destruction. In contrast, anyone who has taken even the first faltering steps in learning the ABC of spiritual science is aware that every lie is a murder at the level of soul. The aeroplane bombs which caused the tragic destruction of human lives and buildings were accompanied by a gigantic project of mental deception in the form of the Pearl Harbor comparison. This lie was enlisted because it had proven 'successful' since the Second World War, and unknowingly wormed its way into the souls of millions of people.

The testimony of the former CIA chief William Casey

As the Japanese storm began to gather force in the Pacific, the most private communications between the Japanese government and its ambassadors in Washington, Berlin, Rome and other major capitals were being read in Washington. Army and navy cryptographers, having broken the Japanese diplomatic cipher, were reading messages that foretold the attack. The British had sent word that a Japanese fleet was steaming east towards Hawaii.

The Secret War Against Hitler, Washington 1988, p. 7. Casey's memoirs were published a year after his death

---

But how should the world come to some clarity about a catastrophe if, from the very outset, it is 'explained' by means of a catastrophic and destructive lie, which remains opaque to most people?

What does it mean when old patriotic ideas and feelings linked to a gigantic untruth are led over into *new* patriotic feelings born of horror and sadness in the face of the New York catastrophe? It means that new ideas and feelings are burdened by a great weight of old ideas and moods built on illusion and deception. It means that a mighty edifice of lies corrupts feelings of genuine compassion, eating its way through souls like a deadly corrosive. It means the dimming of consciousness in a population that needs to be as awake as possible to digest and come to terms with the 'unthinkable'.

On 30 January 1917, Rudolf Steiner said the following in relation to the activity of certain western secret societies:

> It is indeed a significant magical sleight of hand to spread untruth through the world in such a way that it works as truth.

This, he says, actually enables occult influence on politics to achieve far more than mere lies, in the face of which one can still experience a certain healthy distrust. For,

> ...this effect of 'untruth as truth' contains an enormous force of evil. And this force of evil is made full use of in various ways and by different interests.[9]

4. 'Wonderful results'

But the latter is only possible if people's awareness has been dimmed and lulled to sleep. The worst 'sleepers' are therefore not underground cells, the candidates for future terrorist suicide missions, but the millions of sleepers who, confronted by events such as recent ones, lapse into an emotional nightmare of hatred and fear instead of trying to look the facts full in the face with a wakeful, fearless sense of truth.

HOW WE WERE TRICKED INTO WORLD WAR II

FDR
THE OTHER SIDE
OF THE COIN

Hamilton Fish, LL. D.

Franklin Delano Roosevelt and a critical work

Such 'sleepers' included all the European heads of state, above all the Germans, who, as though in a collective knee-jerk reaction, gave the American government—I specifically don't say 'the Americans', among whom I number some very good friends who would most like to protect every decent human being against their own government—a blank cheque for immeasurable global revenge and retaliation.

As such, these sleepers have decisively contributed to realizing a long-term political project of the West. Nothing, since the fall of the Berlin Wall, has so advanced the 'Euro-American' project as did the almost idiotic announcements of solidarity with the future aims of the US administration by NATO heads of state. The Euro-America constructed in the schematic *Economist* map (see p. 23) in September 1990 has now reached the stage where the political cement culturally, politically and militarily binding the 'Christian' (Catholic or Protestant) part of Europe with the USA can be fixed in place and solidified. No event so sharply divided Slav-dominated Eurasia from Euro-America as September 11. No event so massively advanced establishment of the 'Islamistan' block as September 11. And no event—as the hypnotized statesmen of Europe stood by and applauded—secured the US government such dominance of its own jurisdiction over all national legislative structures as September 11. It was also this same event which, more than anything else, secured the USA's geopolitical control (over oil above all) in important areas of the Near East.

For long-term western policies do these not represent truly 'wonderful results', as McGeorge Bundy put it?

5. Eleven questions about September 11
Or: Is the Pearl Harbor comparison actually horribly true?

Following the sad events of September 11, 2001, and in view of the deceitful Pearl Harbor policy of 1941—enlisted as comparison by the US itself—would it not be dozy and naïve to simply assume that these events, too, were a total 'surprise', as all the court media insist?[10]

A few questions can preserve the unprejudiced observer from over-hasty acceptance of the assurances so loudly and frequently repeated, and give him pause for thought:

1) Are there any reasonable grounds to assume that President Bush, whose father was, like William Casey, chief of the CIA for many years, and others such as Kissinger and Brzezinski, were unaware of the true nature of the Pearl Harbor catastrophe?

2) Why is it that the whole world can observe the dire news being whispered into Bush's ear on screen in front of pupils at the elementary school in Florida (see picture on p. 31)?

3) For such a grave piece of news would the President not have been called aside to hear the information in private, giving him the opportunity to take it in alone in the first instance, instead of in front of the world's media?

4) Why were the attacks not prevented, despite the fact that the FBI was hot on the tail of the two alleged chiefs of the operation, Mohamed Atta and Marwan al-Shehhi, and in the 12 hours beforehand had kept them under almost continual surveillance (see picture on p. 58)?

5) How was it that immediately after the attacks *almost everything* was known about the background, training location, etc. of the attackers?

6) Why did neither Bush nor Cheney, nor any other leading members of the administration, seriously censure the security forces for this catastrophic failure?

7) Or was it not a failure?

8) What led President Bush to announce an 'Asiatic fleet memorial day' on 7 June, 2001, and at the same time remember the attack on Pearl Harbor,

which 'pushed America into the Second World War'?

9) What led President Bush to pay an official visit to the CIA's headquarters in Langley, Virginia, on 26 September 2001—the second during his tenure in office—and, in jovial mood, as the cameras were rolling, to offer CIA chief George Tenet and the assembled staff his profound thanks for the work they had achieved so far? And to do so without the slightest inference of blame in relation to the events of September 11, but rather to speak repeatedly of the new war. His actual words were: *'September 11th is a sad memory, but it's a memory [...] And I can't thank you enough on behalf of the American people.'*[11]

10) Why did Bush declare 6 October to be 'German-American Day'?

11) Are there any grounds for assuming that Bush's policies (like those of his father who started the first Gulf War under a deceptive pretext[12]) need less lubrication with lies than those of Roosevelt? The shameless appeal to Pearl Harbor already proves the opposite. Or—still more shamelessly—was a terrible truth actually being expressed openly?

One doesn't need to be a so-called conspiracy theorist to ask such questions. One just needs to give serious attention to the role the President played before, during and after the events of September 11. One just needs to give serious thought to what leading individuals in American politics have cited as the most important precedent to September 11 in American history.

6. Seeking the right attitude to evil

Anyone who makes a sober and reflective attempt to understand the September 11 catastrophe, which is thus also a catastrophe of untruth and lies, must find an objective stance from which to regard evil. We are unable to do this so long as we *hate* bin Laden, terrorism in general or also the American or any other government, or as long as we allow ourselves to succumb to *fear* in response to the latest reports of possible biological terrorism etc. We need to learn to see the extent to which evil is only ever *permitted* by the spiritual powers which hold sway in the world, to which even the most evil dictatorship is subject. Mephistopheles, in the Prologue to Goethe's *Faust*, 'is *compelled* to work as devil', so that human activity should never 'grow lame'. We need to see that there is no *absolute* or *eternal* evil in the universe. However dire the forms of evil, however much it rages, it is still part of evolution in so far as it is spatial and temporal in nature. *Eternal* evil does not exist any more than a square circle.

To ascribe an enduring or eternal nature to evil can profit certain evil powers, and benefit their activity for a time; for this endows evil with a power which one can easily come to fear. It becomes 'unbounded', 'endless', perhaps 'unconquerable'. Those who *fear* or *hate* evil are unable to observe and evaluate its objective existence and its role within all evolution.

Lies are the evil of the intellect; immorality is the evil of the will. However, the one can subtly shift into the other, for lying is also based on an act of will, and, vice

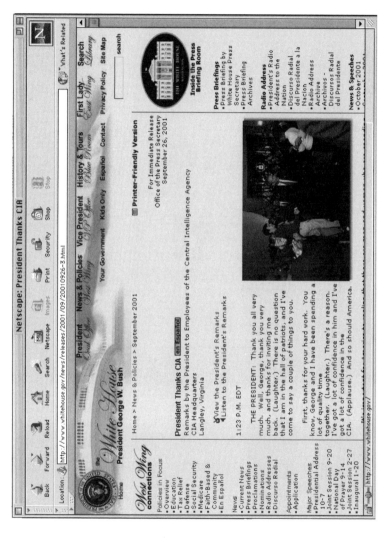

Document dated 26.9.2001 from the White House website

AMERICA / *Deceptive Routines*

Tracking the Terrorists   The movements of Mohamed Atta and Abdulaziz Alomari in and around Portland, Maine, before the World Trade Center attacks.

Monday, Sept. 10

5:43 p.m.
COMFORT INN, SOUTH
PORTLAND

Atta and
Alomari
check in.

8:05 p.m.
PIZZA HUT, SOUTH PORTLAND

Screaming from 6 to 9 p.m. two
Middle Eastern man are seen.

8:31 p.m.
KEY BANK AUTOMATED TELLER
MACHINE, SOUTH PORTLAND

Both men were photographed by
drive-up ATM
driving a blue
2001 Nissan
Altima rental
car with a
Massachusetts
license plate,
3335VII.

8:41 p.m.
FAST GREEN ATM,
SOUTH PORTLAND

Both men
photographed at
an ATM located
in the parking lot
of Pizzeria Uno.

9:15 p.m.
JETPORT GAS
STATION,
SOUTH-
PORTLAND

Both men
photographed.
Atta is wearing
a light-and
dark-colored
shirt.

9:22 p.m.
WAL MART, SCARBOROUGH

Both men photographed
entering the store and
exiting
about 20
minutes
later.

Tuesday, Sept. 11

5:33 a.m.
COMFORT INN SOUTH,
PORTLAND

Atta and Alomari
check out.

5:43 a.m.
PORTLAND
INTERNATIONAL AIRPORT,
S. PORTLAND

Blue 2001 Nissan Altima
enters and parks on the
first floor directly across
from the airport
entrance.

5:40 a.m.
PORTLAND INTERNATIONAL AIRPORT.

Both men check in at U.S. Airways
counter.

5:45 a.m.
PORTLAND
INTERNATIONAL
AIRPORT

Both men pass
through airport
security.

6 a.m.
PORTLAND INTERNATIONAL AIRPORT

Both men depart on Colgan Air en
route to Boston.

Source: Federal Bureau of Investigation

INTERNATIONAL HERALD TRIBUNE, SATURDAY-SUNDAY, OCTOBER 6-7, 2001   PAGE 3

Terrorists' Last Night: Fast Food and Shopping in Maine

The movements of the alleged hijackers were surveyed in detail by the FBI (International Herald Tribune) versa, the intellect can help immorality achieve great guile and ingenuity.

Radically conquering fear and hatred of evil is a fundamental prerequisite for coming to terms with it in both an epistemological and moral sense. Sad contemporary events thus pose a great challenge to each one of us. Considering the following core idea by Rudolf Steiner may be the best help of all in confronting this challenge:

> *Everything in the universe is good, and evil only exists for a limited period. That is why only those who confuse the temporal with the eternal believe in everlasting evil; and that is why those who do not ascend from the temporal to the eternal can never learn to understand evil.*[13]

By repeatedly reflecting on this distinction between time and eternity and the distinction connected to it between soul and spirit; by meditatively pondering on it time and again, we can acquire a stance which, in response to the cauldron of emotions all too easily stirred up by contemporary events, gradually enables us both to observe more dispassionately and, however limited in scope, play a helping part in the course of these events.

The caricature above was published in 1945 in The New Yorker. *The* Europäer *caricaturist tried to show what it might mean to take the 9/11–Pearl Harbor comparison seriously . . . (see opposite page)*

Mr. President, THE EVENT has just occurred. Now please appear surprised! Good luck!

Oh... eh... what was it my advisors said about THE EVENT? 'First of all say nothing—that's really effective! The important thing is not to give the game away by grinning. All depends on the first few moments. The rest will follow by itself.'

4

September 11, 2001 and Pearl Harbor

Conclusions from a widely broadcast comparison

On the evening of September 11, 2001, President Bush dictated into a war diary: 'Today the Pearl Harbor of the 21st century took place.'[1]

The comparison with the Japanese attacks on the US Pacific base of Pearl Harbor made by the Americans immediately after the September 11 attacks is not just a passing whim, but highly indicative of the whole September 11 issue and its global political consequences. It had a decisive impact on the work of the official investigative commission, and informed public awareness throughout the world.

'A purple American fury'

To every average American the words 'Pearl Harbor' conjure an image of President Roosevelt standing up in Congress and speaking with pathos and indignation of this *Day of Infamy,* in order to urge his hitherto reluctant nation to mount a military campaign against Japan and Nazi Germany—with success, as history shows.

This parallel was also drawn by Zbigniew Brzezinski and other influential office-holders or US government insiders. In the week following the attacks, *Time* magazine issued the following appeal in heavy bold print to every American citizen:

What's needed is a unified, unifying sort of purple American fury—a ruthless indignation that doesn't leak away in a week or two.[2]

This appeal pulled the scab from the only comparable traumatic wound in the awareness of the American people, the only one it had ever previously sustained.

In the same way as after Pearl Harbor, the whole nation suddenly stood united behind its President—this time behind one who until then, largely due to misjudged private investments and public speech slip-ups, had been cast in a poor light. Tub-thumping polemic satisfied the public mood. Precise statements about the perpetrators and events leading up to the attacks were superfluous. On with the crusade against Islamic terrorism!

Court literature or independent research?

In general, as for all important historical events, there are two types of literature relating to the Japanese attack on Pearl Harbor: 'court literature' studies on which the comparison with September 11 is based, which are dependent on the interests of those currently in power and reach academic circles via the popular media; and studies by independent historians and commentators which inevitably cast this event in a quite different light.

Independent research shows that the attack was provoked by the Roosevelt administration in a series of political and economic steps. The specific location of the attack was known to the US government months beforehand, and its date a week in advance, since it had cracked the Japanese code. However, *relevant* information relating to the imminent attack was withheld from those in command on Hawaii, General Short and Admiral Kimmel. The untrue account of events there, broadcast by the media on 8 December 1941, transformed Congress's and the US people's previous refusal to enter the war into instantaneous and universal support for a military commitment.

Those who think that Roosevelt's sacrifice of 3,000 US citizens was absolutely justified, since it served as a means to a righteous end—liberating the world from Nazism—might like to consider that the latter had previously been significantly aided in its rise by US funding and policies.[3] Let me mention here the independent *American* Pearl Harbor researchers: George Morgenstern, Charles A. Beard, Charles C. Tansill, Harry Elmer Barnes, Admiral Kimmel, Hamilton Fish.[4]

Conspiracy literature?
Here I would refer readers too accustomed to the official version, who may by now have lost all patience and are reaching for the 'conspiracy literature' cudgels, to the book by the American Robert Stinnett, *Day of Deceit, The Truth About FDR and Pearl Harbor.* (The German edition recently published by Zweitausendeins translates as: 'Pearl Harbor, How the American government provoked the attack and allowed 2,476 of its citizens to die.') Even *The New York Times,* which tends to favour the official literature and its journalists, had to admit: 'It is difficult, after reading this copiously documented

book, not to wonder about previously unchallenged assumptions about Pearl Harbor.'[5]

'...it wasn't the Japanese, but it was al Qaeda'

Despite this 'shaking of foundations', the National Commission on Terrorist Attacks Upon the United States, which only belatedly formed in the autumn of 2002 at the urging of the public, still swears on the 'classic' version of events. As early as the first introductory session, leading Commission members lent heavily on a book which no less a figure than Donald Rumsfeld has been pressing into the hands of anyone who crosses his path: the book by Roberta Wohlstetter, *Pearl Harbor, Warning and Decision*,[6] published in the 1960s. Harry Elmer Barnes called Wohlstetter's book exemplary for the method of 'historical blurt-out'. What he means by this is that even by including aspects which directly contradict the basic thesis that the attack was a surprise, it still succeeds in giving this overall impression. Just as after Pearl Harbor so now too, after September 11, we are only supposed to ask: How was it possible for us to be caught unawares? Except that in this instance, in the words of the Commission report, it '...wasn't the Japanese, but it was al Qaeda'.[7]

Albert Wohlstetter, Paul Wolfowitz and Richard Perle

Roberta Wohlstetter, by the way, was the wife of Albert Wohlstetter, a mathematician and one of the spiritual fathers of the Star Wars programme. According to an obituary, Wohlstetter, who died in 1997 at the age of 83, was the 'world's most influential *unknown figure* of the past half century'.[8]

Wohlstetter initiated the idea of preventive attacks using chemical 'smart bombs'. He was the undisputed leader of the 'team of Hawks' which called for military steps based on 'breathtaking creativity and imagination'. Two of his closest protégés were Paul Wolfowitz and Richard Perle. The latter even became his son-in-law. The heritage of the Pearl Harbor lie thus passed for decades through an astonishing circle of influential individuals, acquiring a solid consistency.

Consequences

If Pearl Harbor was a true precedent to September 11, then one must infer that the current administration practises the same unscrupulousness in relation to its citizens as did the Roosevelt government.

If the comparison broadcast by it is taken seriously, this leads, firstly, to a realistic insight into the actual structure of US politics; secondly, it decapitates the Pearl Harbor lie which has, shamelessly, once again been brought into play; and thirdly it smoothes the way for a comprehensive and independent investigation of September 11.

How will the mass population of America regard their government once they awaken from their illusions?

Asking the right questions

No reasonable person will deny that the Japanese attacked Hawaii in 1941. But the US administration could have mitigated the attack or even thwarted it, thus sparing the lives of its own citizens. That it did not do so was due to its ambitions for global power. In the case of September 11, likewise, the question is not: 'Was it the al Qaeda Islamic group?' but rather: 'Who was really in control?' (And this control may have lain elsewhere altogether.) By spreading the Pearl Harbor comparison, the leading figures in American power politics have themselves thrown open this question, rather than any so-called 'conspiracy theorists'.

The chief service of authors such as Gerhard Wisnewski, Andreas von Bülow, Michael C. Ruppert, Nafeez Ahmed, Gore Vidal, Thierry Meyssan and many others is that they have not given up on this question, even if they may not be always accurate in every detail.

5

'Dishonesty as a fundamental characteristic of our time'

Notes on the current world situation

Dishonesty as basic trait of public life

As long ago as 1920 Rudolf Steiner commented that 'dishonesty is the fundamental characteristic of all public life in our time'.[1] This basic trait has become still more dominant since, above all in political life. Hitlerism was built on lies, as was Bolshevism. American political life was built on lies in the past and is still today. After the collapse of the systems of deception mentioned above, the 'only global superpower' (Zbigniew Brzezinski) is now, one can say, in pole position in the lying stakes.

The principle of targeted provocation

In what follows I would like to cite a few facts about US policies and their *anti-American* character, for these policies are, not least, deceiving and damaging the US's own citizens.[2]

- The Japanese attack on Pearl Harbor (7 December 1941) which, as we know, led to the USA's entry into the Second World War, was in complete contrast to official accounts not a surprise attack but one the Roosevelt administration intentionally provoked, using the 'Day of Infamy' to put the USA's Congress and people in a mood for war. The American writer and commentator Gore Vidal speaks of a 'barefaced lie', going on to say that Roosevelt, whose domestic policies and New Deal he admires, provoked the Japanese intentionally in order to get them to attack.[3]

- The 'Gulf of Tonking incident' (2 August 1964) brought about the sudden, swift expansion of the Vietnam War. Two North Vietnamese torpedo boats are said to have attacked the American destroyer *Maddox*. This 'incident' led to the Tonking Resolution in the Security Council, triggering the wholesale bombardment of North Vietnam. The torpedo 'incident' was a pure invention by the USA. Interestingly, the news was broadcast via AP from *Pearl Harbor*.[4]

- Zbigniew Brzezinski boasted in an interview that it was the CIA which supported the rebels against Moscow in Afghanistan, and thus enticed the Russians into their 'Vietnam'.

- The US ambassador April Glaspie assured the Iraqi government on 25 July 1990 that the USA would not intervene in the Iraq-Kuwait conflict. After the invasion of Kuwait the US government lodged a fierce protest and threatened to intervene.

- On 10 October 1990, the daughter of the Kuwaiti ambassador appeared before the human rights committee of Congress and, choking back tears, reported on atrocities perpetrated by Iraqi soldiers in Kuwait. The 'incubator' story was born: Iraqi soldiers, she said, had dragged hundreds of babies from incubators and cast them to a tortured death. Behind this story stood a ten million dollar commission to America's biggest Public Relations company Hill & Knowlton. Amnesty International later corrected this 'error'. But by then the anti-Iraqi mood had been kindled, and led two days later to the Iraq Resolution in the Security Council: a green light for the first Gulf War.

From Pearl Harbor to September 11

On the very day of the New York catastrophe the comparison with the attack on Pearl Harbor was drawn, initially probably in the President's aeroplane Airforce One, then also by Brzezinski and others. This emotionally stirring parallel, which was immediately trumpeted abroad by the media, could have made all who knew the real facts about Pearl Harbor—and not just the 'official version' or the Hollywood film released in the summer of 2001—prick up their ears. (And so could the tangible links between the CIA, Pakistan's secret service, al Qaeda and the funding given to Mohamed Atta, the chief highjacker; or the substantial business links between the Bush and bin Laden families.)

It was in fact absolutely right to compare September 11 and Pearl Harbor, for such a comparison is appallingly accurate. As Kennedy and Johnson adviser McGeorge Bundy's callous commentary put it in relation to the increase in US power resulting from Pearl Harbor, it was a 'dreadful day but had a really wonderful result'.[5]

'Dealing in straight power concepts'

Whoever wants to grasp the basic character of US foreign policy implicit in such words need only read the guidelines, treated as top secret for decades, which George Kennan, director of the US foreign ministry's planning department, set out in 1948. In Kennan's 'Planning study 23' it is stated:

> [...] we have about 50% of the world's wealth but only 6.3% of its population. [...] In this situation, we cannot fail to be the object of envy and resentment. Our real task in the coming period is to devise a pattern of relationships which will permit us to maintain this position of disparity without positive detriment to our national security. To do so, we will have to dispense with all sentimentality and day-dreaming; and our attention will have to be concentrated everywhere on our immediate national objectives. We need not deceive ourselves that we can afford today the luxury of altruism and world-bene-faction. [...] We should cease to talk about vague and—for the Far East—unreal objectives such as human rights, the raising of living standards, and democratization. The day is not far off when we are going to have to deal in straight power concepts. The less we are then hampered by idealistic slogans, the better.[6]

Here, for once, the thrust of US foreign policy was blatantly revealed.

The first US war without a pretext

Whoever reckons with the impetus of such guidelines

will not be surprised at the way the sole superpower is currently dealing with 'human rights' or the UN's humanitarian aims and its 'idealistic slogans'. The current war is evidence of the dismal advance of US policy in the last 50 years. It has now really reached the point in which it no longer allows itself to be inhibited by 'idealistic slogans'.

Almost a joke
America is at this moment developing advanced systems of 'weapons of mass destruction' and is prepared to use them where it sees fit. It has more of them than the rest of the world put together. It has walked away from international agreements on biological and chemical weapons, refusing to allow inspection of its own factories. The hypocrisy behind its public declarations and its own actions is almost a joke.

Harold Pinter, playwright, addressing the House of Commons, October 2002

Certainly, Saddam Hussein's actions were despicable. The CIA was also aware of this when it started to support and use him at the end of the 60s. US policy exploits useful villains everywhere as part of its technique. Hussein is a son of a bitch, went the phrase at the time, but he is *our* son of a bitch. Since the end of the 80s he is no longer 'our' son of a bitch. That is the whole difference. That is his cardinal crime and why he must go, even if this costs the lives of thousands of civilians. This is acting according to 'straight power concepts'.

The sole superpower thus for the first time set a war in motion without having fabricated any *credible* moral garment to cloak it in, and without *successfully* mobilizing the public's moral indignation. This is the new and frightening thing about the current world situation. The regime with the worst weapons of mass destruction on the planet is threatening the safety of the whole world. This is all the more mendacious if the unrestrained US junta, in pseudo-moral pose, seeks to present its wars of world dominion as the legitimate outpouring of divine apocalyptic fury.

Towards a free exchange of information

We can only oppose such developments by looking them clearly in the eye, and by ensuring we are not befuddled by 'idealistic' or pseudo-religious 'slogans'. To do so we need to develop a life of intellect and spirit focused on truth. At the level of public reporting this would mean creating an independent exchange of information. (During the First World War in Zurich, Rudolf Steiner wanted to set up a *neutral* information office, a plan thwarted by the German OHL [army command]).

There would certainly be an opportunity to do something like this in Europe. Additionally, despite its flotsam and jetsam of irrelevant material, the world wide web allows unchecked international exchange of information and the circulation of independent views. One can speak of the beginning of an alternative, autonomous web-press. A not insignificant proportion of the global protest against the official version of 9/11 did not draw its factual and critical information from the mainstream press but from internet sources.

6

Michael C. Ruppert—an American seeker of truth

Michael C. Ruppert was born in 1951 to a family with very close links to America's political, military and secret service sphere. His father was a pilot in the Korean war, his mother worked in an army code-breaking department, relatives of his father worked for the OSS, a forerunner of the Central Intelligence Agency founded in 1947, and then also for the CIA itself. Already as a boy he realized, through his mother's work, that the Japanese bombardment of Pearl Harbor on 7 December 1941 was not a surprise attack. Since both the military and navy codes of the Japanese had been cracked with the help of the British, he was aware of the main preparatory stages leading up to the attack, which the Roosevelt administration had intentionally provoked.

Ruppert studied politics and graduated with honours in 1973 from the University of California (UCLA). Following this he worked in the anti-drugs section of the Los Angeles police department.

In 1977, while doing some research, he discovered that the CIA was involved in drug trafficking. When Ruppert tried to go public with his discovery, he met resistance. Initially attempts were made to entice him into becoming a CIA 'case officer' (top level of the extensive CIA hierarchy). When Ruppert refused to acquiesce to this, he lost his job, despite the fact that he had received

Michael C. Ruppert

outstanding commendations for his work and there were no disciplinary proceedings pending against him. He had to wait 18 years before he succeeded in confronting John Deutch, the CIA director of the time, about this during a national public TV broadcast in relation to three specific CIA drugs projects. With his rambling, sloganistic assurances of the truth, Deutch's credibility was so damaged that he had to pay for this appearance by sacrificing his nomination for the post of defence minister in the Clinton administration.

Since 1998 Ruppert has produced the internet journal *From The Wilderness*, which now has thousands of subscribers in 32 countries, including members of the

US Congress and university professors. It publishes reports about the current world situation written by himself or colleagues. In the past Ruppert has focused particular attention on the role of the billions of dollars, obtained from illicit drug dealing (via the Wall Street bankers who control it), that shore up the American economy.

'The Third Reich just changed venues...'
On 28 November 2001, Ruppert addressed over 1,000 students at Portland State University (Oregon) for more than two hours about 'The Truth and Lies of 9-11'. This lecture was recorded and can be ordered as video cassette or DVD from www.copvcia.com. I mention this here because it really is an extraordinary document, the summation of decades of research, which analyses the events of 11 September against a broad background of political, secret service and financial dealings. Ruppert avoids speculation and bases his assessments and diagnoses on actual government documents, public statements, verifiable press reports and published books. He starts by forcefully drawing his listeners' attention to the fact that their freedom is at risk, that their citizens' rights are under extreme threat and in fact have already been largely revoked since various emergency laws were passed in response to September 11. On 26 October 2002, Bush junior signed the 'USA/Patriot Act' as a so-called anti-terror measure.[1] This law, which was not even submitted to the House of Representatives in printed form prior to the forced vote, permits dwellings

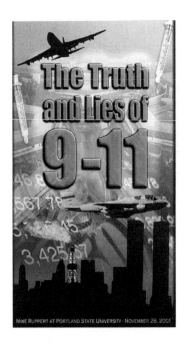

MIKE RUPPERT AT PORTLAND STATE UNIVERSITY · NOVEMBER 28, 2001

or business premises to be searched in the absence of residents, and owners to be compelled to secrecy about such searches. Furthermore it permits monitoring of a US citizen's internet traffic without a warrant, based on nothing more than mere suspicion, interception of his e-mails, and surveillance of telephone calls made from public call boxes. Such things are, it is true, not new in practice. What is new is that the information acquired by such means can now be used in court as evidence. The law does contain a clause that is meant to calm the fears of many citizens, with the fine name of 'sunset clause', which creates a sense that these emergency measures are of limited duration. In fact it is made clear that such measures can be used outside the period of a particular terrorist emergency, 'where investigations of a foreign secret service are underway that began *prior* to the time at which the measures are to be cancelled'.

On 9 November 2001—a day of great historical import which was to acquire notorious publicity in relation to the history of the Third Reich[2]—Justice Minister Ashcroft issued a decree permitting surveillance of conversations between a solicitor and his client where the latter was suspected of perpetrating a terrorist attack.

On 13 November 2001 Bush issued a further emergency decree, permitting foreigners suspected of being terrorists to be brought before a military tribunal. Such proceedings are conducted in secret, and prosecutors do not have to produce evidence if 'this is in the interests of national security'. The death sentence can be applied in these cases, 'even if a third of officers present' are against this.

One might reflect here whether, for instance, overhearing a foreigner raising objections to the legitimacy of the 'Patriot Act' in a New York café might not be sufficient grounds to have him hauled before such a tribunal...

*

In his commentary Ruppert also presents a detailed chronicle of events leading up to September 11 (from 1991 to 2001), and considers the period following it (up to 28 August 2002). He includes a recording of the debate with John Deutch as well as interviews with various members of Congress and financial experts.

The brilliant highpoint of his account in relation to US foreign policy of recent decades is an analysis of the main theses of Brzezinski's book *The Grand Chessboard* (1997). Ruppert not only clearly reveals the US's Eurasian-focused geopolitical programme, but also uncovers the arrogant will to power which relegates all of non-American humanity to the status of US vassals or underdeveloped barbarians. The lecture, illustrated by charts, culminates in the reference to Brzezinski's concern that, in America's multi-cultural society, it might become ever more difficult to find a general consensus for what he regards as the US's essential geostrategic goal, 'except in the circumstances of a truly massive and widely perceived direct external threat'.[3]

Following this quote from Brzezinski, Ruppert fades in an image of Osama bin Laden. Then he turns to the whole audience and says emphatically: 'I want you to know that the Third Reich did not lose the Second World War. It just changed venues.' If such a thing is said by an American citizen, who genuinely suffers from his nation's domestic and foreign policy, who is seeking the truth and has demonstrated what sacrifices he is prepared to make on behalf of it, then non-Americans also have an objective reason to take such a statement seriously. In a way that may alienate some, Ruppert here makes a link between Nazism and political Americanism, one which may well require the insights of anthroposophical spiritual science for its deeper understanding.[4]

Ruppert certainly did not make this comment in order

to demonize his country but to show that the American people 'may be ruled by a syndicate of criminals', as the Democrat member of Congress Cynthia McKinney puts it in an interview included by Ruppert in his tape.

7

G.W.F. Hegel's dual path in the West

Hegel's view of evolution as basis for western politics and esoteric development

Truth is the whole
G.W.F Hegel (1770–1831)

I.

On several occasions the *Europäer* magazine has drawn attention to the fact that Anglo-American political practice is largely based on Central European epistemology: on Hegel's recognition that *all development in the world takes place in the form of contradictory motions,* is actually founded on contrasting opposites.[1] The extreme poles of such contrast are termed 'being and nothingness' in Hegel's philosophy, and he regards all development and evolution as a synthesis of these two poles.[2] Evolution as 'the unity of being and nothingness' is, according to Hegel, the 'prime truth'. In every actual process of development, he says, one can demonstrate the 'moments' when something emerges or arises (as transition from nothingness to being) and fades (as transition from being to nothingness).[3] Thus the contrasting opposites of being and nothing (as 'thesis' and 'antithesis') are united in development (as 'synthesis'). The further result of this development, and that alone, is what Hegel regards as 'existence'.

The only difficulty with this Hegelian concept is that many people tend to want to form and retain nothing but a 'positive' concept of development, consisting of a one-sided 'moment' of emergence alone. This habit of thought leaves the 'moment' of decline aside, without which real development is impossible. For instance, how is 'development' regarded in the commercial sphere? As growth and more growth: continually increasing value with, as far as possible, avoidance of devaluation. This is the credo of entrepreneurs and shareholders. However, reality corrects all our one-sided efforts. In the commercial sphere it intervenes as inflation, unemployment, impoverishment of the masses etc.—in other words at a quite different level, apparently, than where a globalization elite is trying to ensure nothing but 'positive growth'. But from a Hegelian view, one-sided growth and financial recession etc. are phenomena which go hand in hand.[4]

While most Central Europeans have either disregarded the truth of the polar and contradictory character of all development in the world (or in 'existence') or accorded it, at most, a theoretical value only, in the last two centuries it has actually become the foundation of Anglo-American political practice. For this practice the political stances of 'left' and 'right' are for instance not *absolute* positions, one of which should be striven for and the other dismissed or combated. Rather they can be viewed as pole and counter-pole, or thesis and antithesis, both of which need to be cultivated simultaneously or in succession if the interplay of *both* is to give rise to something new (synthesis). It can thus seem very useful to strive for peace and war simulta-

Nach Drakes Basrelief gezeichnet u. gestochen von K. Barth in Hildburghausen

neously in a region, as, on closer examination, US policy actually does in all the theatres of war or crisis regions in the world which it controls.[5] Where links are formed with both or all parties to the conflict, the 'new synthesis' thus aimed at does not by any means have to be peace. It can equally be a growth of what is regarded as necessary power, which is to be achieved in a certain region of the world through an intentionally contradictory policy.[6] Tireless mediation and negotiation with the conflicting parties can even lend such a striving for power the appearance of peace-brokering. A peace-loving person, who regards Hegel as just an abstract European philosopher, without any impact on the world of 'action', will generally view such an appearance at its face value and understandably praise such 'efforts at peace', even if they regularly evaporate and lead nowhere, or provide nothing but new fuel for further conflicts.[7]

Western secret services also practise this type of polarity process. European leftwing terrorism in the 70s offers an example of this. In order to combat the leftwing tendencies of European movements, 'leftwing' violence was cultivated, that is, terrorism was supported. This evoked a counter-response in the form of state repression, which was the real goal.[8] Because 'educated' Europeans have lost sight of Hegel in their world view, it was all the easier to use his philosophy in the West as the unacknowledged foundations of *power* politics.

II

But Hegel did not just live on in the Anglo-American West as a misused 'adviser' to power politics. As the British Empire flourished in England his view of development also became the foundation of an esoteric path of schooling of general human significance, and without any vested interest objectives. I am referring to the short book *Light on the Path,* which was first published in 1885. The author Mabel Collins (1851–1927) was a well-known writer and had on occasion worked closely with H.P. Blavatsky. Besides *Light on the Path,* she wrote several works with a spiritual content, including the important novel *Flita.*

Light on the Path can show all who have spiritual aspirations that even an esotericist's soul-spiritual

Mabel Collins (1851–1927)

Rudolf Steiner (1861–1925)

development must be fundamentally based on Hegel's insight into the contradictory nature of all evolution, if one is to avoid certain one-sided tendencies inimical to higher development.

The exercises in *Light on the Path* are systematically structured so as to avoid, or repeatedly overcome, one-sided development: for every main exercise there is a kind of counter-exercise.

The first instruction is to 'Kill out ambition'. The polar exercise to this is 'Work as those work who are ambitious'. Anyone who tried to follow the first exercise alone might considerably lame his energies. Those on the other hand who only pursued the second might dangerously enhance the personal ambition present in all of us.

Neither the first nor the second exercise are, on their own, the significant thing. What is important is what *develops* in the soul as a result of practising this apparently contradictory pair of exercises. This is not expressed and does not need to be. Each person has to experience for himself the unexpressed result and synthesis of both exercises.

The following exercises are also built on this contradictory structure. 'Kill out all sense of separateness' says another instruction; 'Yet stand alone and isolated', is the counter-exercise. 'Seek the way by retreating within', urges another main exercise; 'Seek the way by advancing boldly without' says the complementary instruction. And, to give one last example: 'Desire only that which is within you' and 'Desire only that which is beyond you'.

In this short text the same creative principle—that is, of contradiction leading to real development—is made fruitful in a quite different way from its use in Anglo-American politics. Here too it does not remain philosophical in nature but is applied to practical activity, although in this case the arena of activity is not the stage of external world events but the soul of each individual.

All military conflicts, which are the very lifeblood of the political machinations referred to, are here internalized and resolved within each individual soul. Those who enter *this* arena of conflict will soon see that all outer conflicts, battles or wars are in reality nothing but unresolved soul conflicts projected outwards. All external killing then appears as a caricature of the killing which is legitimately practised in the human soul. For here, on the inner battlefield of the soul, the human ego may and in fact should learn to kill without compunction. Killing means to withdraw life from something. Soul impulses can also acquire life. When this happens they become soul *properties* over time. Killing in the inner arena of the soul is meant quite literally: it involves uprooting certain soul properties such as ambition, 'sense of separateness' etc. from the *life body* where they have become anchored over time and thus become *habits*. The life from which these attributes live parasitically must, in a very real sense, be withdrawn from them.

To the extent to which someone enters the inner arena of conflicts and in the above sense practises and accomplishes 'contradictory' things, he will not only advance his own soul and spiritual development but also contribute to lasting peace in the external world: a peace that is neither achieved through peace negotiations nor can be destroyed by military actions.

III.

Whereas the fundamental tendency in western politics is ultimately underpinned by aims and motives opposed to what is universally human, instead advancing the large-scale yet nevertheless personal ambitions of a relatively small number of influential people, the esoteric schooling offered in *Light on the Path* stresses the extreme importance of full, unrestricted knowledge and the overcoming of ambitious personal motives. This is clear, for instance, from the seventeenth 'rule' and the remark about it. The instruction to 'Seek out the way' may, after the previous 16 'rules', appear somewhat terse and paradoxical. The following commentary is appended to it:

These four words seem, perhaps, too slight to stand alone. The disciple may say, Should I study these thoughts at all? Did I not seek out the way? Yet do not pass on hastily. Pause and consider awhile. Is it the *way* you desire, or is it that there is a dim perspective in your visions of great heights to be scaled by *yourself*, of a great future for *you* to compass? Be warned. The way is to be sought for its own sake, not with regard to *your* feet that shall tread it [italics by T.M.].

IV.

In *Central Europe* Hegel really only had one significant successor: Rudolf Steiner. Steiner once called Hegel the greatest philosopher in world history.[9] A bust of Hegel given to him in Weimar travelled with him to his later homes in Berlin and Dornach. But Steiner also placed Hegel's philosophy in a broad continuum of evolution by showing that he represented the culmination and conclusion of a philosophical system built on the element of abstract thinking, and that, in world historical terms, a transition was needed from abstract thinking to the specific experiences of supersensible perception. 'I find no difference between my outlook and that of Hegel,' he wrote in a letter to Eduard von Hartmann on 1 November 1894, 'but merely draw certain consequences from him.'[10] One of these consequences is that he did not, as did Hegel, base his philosophy on the *concept,* but on the *actual activity of thinking* which first has to make all concepts manifest.[11] Steiner drew a second consequence with his appeal that Hegelian philosophy should penetrate like yeast the spiritual science he founded. He once stressed this forcefully in the following words:

There is a certain power, certainly not a physical power, but another kind of force, a spiritual force in this Hegelian approach. In it lies something that must be taken up by every spiritual world view. Spiritual science would become rachitic if not penetrated by the bony skeleton of ideas that Hegel wrested from

Ahriman, from calcifying Ahriman.[12] [...] One needs this dispassionate capacity to reflect if one wishes not to lose one's way in a warm fog of mysticism when engaged in spiritual research.[13]

This appeal is also a direct consequence of Hegelian thinking: what has once been achieved through human evolution as a capacity for pure, objective thinking, must not be lost. It must be retained as a 'preserved element' in all further development.[14]

The third consequence which Steiner drew from Hegel is that he also rendered Hegel's insight into the dialectics of all development fruitful for spiritual scientific training. At the beginning of the 20th century he used Mabel Collins's short book as a core starting point of specific esoteric instruction for his pupils, in the sphere of practical occultism.

In relation to the last example cited above from Collins's book ('Desire only that which lives within you' etc.), Steiner commented on 15 February 1904:

You may ask whether you really need both phrases, and if so why. Yes, indeed, we need both [...] We must practise them so that we do not understand a truth from a one-sided perspective, but view the world from all angles [...] Life always alternates between good and evil, between beauty and ugliness and so forth. These are things that always contradict each other. We will only come to know the life of spirit if we do not get caught up in the details, if we don't take offence at contradictions, but understand that contradictions are the very essence of life. In this way we practise control of our own thoughts. Then we can always be aware that once we have grasped an idea we must immediately seek the other, opposite idea that belongs to it, which relates to the first as hunger to satiety. By this means one aspect of the idea will be enhanced by its opposite, as light and shadow, as positive and negative enhance each other. Those who observe this will gradually develop the capacity to dwell in living spirituality. They will come to live in a spiritual existence that is higher than the life of the senses.[15]

This is Hegelianism that has been *developed further* in the sphere of practical esoteric training. The fact that Steiner collaborated with Collins in this sphere is like a wonderful counterbalance to the misuse of Hegel by occult political circles in the West. The latter is in fact nothing other than a caricature of the true path which Collins and Steiner developed in the field of practical occultism from the ideas of one of the world's greatest philosophers.

8

What can replace the 'survival of the unfittest' in positions of power?

In the decisive year of 1917 Rudolf Steiner once pointed out that a certain evolutionary development since the beginning of the 15th century was causing some concern to certain individuals with spiritual insight.[1]

He was referring to the fact that people with an authentic striving for spirituality, i.e. those who gradually replace the environmental and educational influences affecting them with ones derived from an inner autonomy and self-education, are usually not very keen on intervening in external social and political matters. In other words, due to their spiritual inclinations and endeavours they prefer to leave political work to others.[2] The inevitable consequence—and the concern referred to—is that politics is left to those who neither seek nor cultivate purely spiritual impulses, but instead can best serve their own group interests. The reluctance to engage in mundane political life of those who try to develop purely spiritual striving *is really the reason why the exercise of power has passed into the hands of people who put everything, including occult traditions of knowledge, at the service of group egotism and vested interests.* Even if the general mood of our times emphasizes public transparency and individual self-determination, the efforts by groups that have come to power in this way focus—in complete contrast—on secrecy (and thus the tendency to create an aristocracy of power) and manipulation of the individual.

The 20th century showed humanity what can happen when public affairs are 'run' or 'managed' almost exclusively by those with no spiritual leanings. It showed us what can arise when, through the passivity of spiritually inclined people in relation to the external affairs of public life, a 'selection of the unfittest' (i.e. of the least spiritual) leads to them occupying positions of power. The beginning of the 21st century has already shown that the catastrophes of the 20th century may be only a foretaste of far worse things to come.

Those who are serious about 'global responsibility' can draw only *one* consequence from past catastrophes of the 20th century and the current world catastrophe: they must help spread insights gained through a science of the spirit, to illumine the context and background to global events in an ever clearer and more *truthful* way.

Then, perhaps already in this century, a growing number of people will want and also be able to regulate economic, cultural and political affairs in a way that draws wholly on spiritual perspectives to take account of *all* humanity. Can there be any other light at the end of the tunnel of violence and lies with which the century began?

Timeline for 9.11.2001

José García Morales

Sequential chronology of the events of September 11, 2001
(Times in brackets are divergent variations.)

7:59 American Airlines (AA) flight 11 (Boeing 767) takes off from Logan airport, Boston, destined for Los Angeles.[1,15]

8:13 Ground station of the FAA (Federal Aviation Administration, civil aviation control) loses contact with Flight 11's transponder.[1]

8:14 United Airlines (UA) flight 175 (Boeing 767) takes off from Logan airport, Boston, destined for Los Angeles (16 minutes late).[1,15]

8:20 Flight (AA) 77 (Boeing 757) takes off from Dulles airport, Washington, destined for Los Angeles (10 minutes late).[1,15]

8:20 Flight 11 deviates from its flight path and is regarded as possibly hijacked.

8:30 Many Bush administration politicians are in their offices by this time and able to receive and pass on information or initiate actions: vice-president Dick Cheney and security adviser Condoleeza Rice in the White House, secretary of defense Donald Rumsfeld in the Pentagon, CIA director Tenet is near the White House, FBI director Mueller is in his office at FBI headquarters.[1]

8:40 (8:38) FAA ground station informs NORAD

(North-American Aerospace Defense Command) that Flight 11 has been hijacked.[1] The secret service (comprising over 4,000 people, who have a far more comprehensive news messaging service than the news agencies[2]) sets up an open line to the ground station and has click-button access to all the USA's radar stations.[1]

This number of staff does not include the NSA secret service (National Security Agency) founded by Truman on 4 November 1952. This agency numbers 38,000 people and possesses extensive technical facilities (e.g. surveillance posts and 90 spy ships on all the world's oceans). It also has greater independence in relation to Congress than the CIA.[3]

Commentary: This means that the secret service is less reliant on the ground station or NORAD passing it further information. At this point information such as this hijack can already be passed to Bush and others. Necessary actions were channelled by the National Military Command Center (NMCC) at the Pentagon, the military command for aircraft hijackings.[1]

8:42 Flight (UA) 93 (Boeing 757) takes off from Newark airport, New York, destined for San Francisco (41 minutes late, planned departure time was 8:01).[1,15]

8:42 Flight 175 deviates from its flight path. The ground station has no further contact with the transponder.[1]

8:43 NORAD (and the secret service) are told that Flight 175 has been hijacked and is flying towards New York.[1]

8:44 Defense minister Rumsfeld speaks in the Pentagon

about terrorism, stressing that: 'There will be another event'.[1]

All the aeroplanes or flights mentioned above disappear from the ground station radar screens for a while. Since there are various reasons to doubt whether the planes reappearing at the strike or crash locations are identical with those which vanished, I assign names to the flights reappearing after their disappearance based on the location they strike, as follows: aircraft World Trade Center 1 (hereafter WTC 1; previously identified as AA 11); aircraft WTC 2 (previously identified as UA 175); aircraft Pentagon (hereafter P; previously identified as AA 77); aircraft Shanksville (hereafter S, previously identified as UA 93). At the very least one would need to check these identities very carefully in each case.

8:46:26 (according to seismographic recordings; other sources give the time as 8:45-8:48) Flight WTC 1 (Flight 11) strikes the North Tower, between the 94th and 98th floors. The aircraft strikes at a slant roughly in the middle of the building's façade.[4]

After 8:46 An open line is set up between NORAD and NMCC.[6]

8:46 General Richard B. Myers, commander-in-chief of the airforce and deputizing general chief of staff is in a meeting with senator Max Cleland, and shortly afterwards hears of this strike on TV but thinks it is just a small aircraft. Until 9:43 he discusses necessary measures with Cleland, but does not ask for further information.[1,2]

8:46 Flight 77 deviates temporarily from its flight path, but NORAD is only informed of this at 9:24. This delay is a grave violation of service regulations.[1]

8:46 Two F-15 fighter planes are ordered to take off from Otis military airport (distance to New York 188 miles) to seek aircraft WTC 1 (Flight 11). This order is not carried out until 8:52, at which point they are looking for aircraft WTC 2 (Flight 175). They reach New York 19 minutes later.[1]

Commentary: Why did they fly so slowly? According to the time cited, their average speed was under 600 mph. If they had flown at 1,600 mph (top speed over 1875 mph) they would have reached New York at 8:59, well before Flight 175 struck the South Tower.[1]

Why did no military airports closer to the scene receive orders?[1] Details about the movements of fighter planes taking off from Otis (for New York) and from Langley military airports (for Washington) were only released by Myers on 14 September. Initially he stated that no fighter planes were scrambled before the strikes. On 13 September, in response to questioning in Congress about why he had done nothing, he still said that he did not know if planes had taken off or not. According to Jared Israel (www.emperors-clothes.com) the scrambling of fighter planes from Otis and Langley is a retrospective fabrication by Myers. Later this became the official version of events ('we tried but we were too late') issued by NORAD. After the attacks Myers was promoted by the President to chief of general staff, that is, supreme commander of US armed forces.[2] (See also 9:27, 9:41).

8:46–8:55 Barbara Olsen's telephone call from Flight P (Flight 77).

Commentary: The problematic nature of this and other telephone calls is addressed by Eric Hufschmid.[4,11]

8:48 First TV news and reports announcing that the first aeroplane has struck the World Trade Center.[1]

8:48 (8:30) Bush's cavalcade of cars leaves his hotel and heads for Emma Booker School in Sarasota (Florida). The distance between the hotel and the school is around five (nine) miles;[1] the distance between the school and airport is five miles.

8:48 Bush is asked by journalist John Cochran whether he knows what is going on in New York. Bush says that he does (ABC News, 11.9.2001).[1,2]

8:55 In the South Tower a loudspeaker announces that 'The building is safe and staff can return to their offices.'

8:55 Flight 77 deviates further from its flight path and flies east towards Washington.[1]

8:56 The ground station loses contact with the Flight 77 transponder. This flight is regarded as missing. NORAD is only informed 28 minutes later.[1]

After 8:56 NMCC officials discuss response actions in the west wing of the Pentagon.

8:58–9:00 Bush arrives at Booker Elementary School, Sarasota.[1]

9:00 This was the time that J. Fullton and his team in the CIA were supposed to carry out an exercise to test conduct of personnel in the case of an aeroplane striking a building. It appears that the exercise was cancelled after the real hijack. The location of the exercise was four miles distant from the airport where one of the four highjacked aeroplanes had just taken off.[5,6]

NORAD was also in the midst of another wargame, named Vigilant Guardian, which was supposed to address an imagined nationwide crisis affecting it. According to statements by a member of staff, 'everyone' at NORAD initially thought that the real highjack was part of the exercise.[5,6] Michael Ruppert's research has shown that the following military exercises (war games) were taking place at the time of the attacks: Vigilant Guardian, Vigilant Warrior, Northern Guardian, Northern Vigilance, and the CIA exercise referred to above. These exercises meant that most fighter planes were withdrawn to the north (Canada, Alaska); on NORAD'S radar screens 22 planes appeared that had deviated from their flight path, some of which were real aircraft and others just simulation on the radar screen. The Joint Chief of Staff, with Myer standing in as active chairman, had organized the Vigilant Warrior exercise with NORAD. This also involved wide-bodied aircraft in US airspace. According to Ruppert, only 8 fighter planes in northeastern USA were available for defence purposes, severely limiting their use in these attacks.[6]

Commentary: Why did Myers, deep in conversation with a senator throughout the attacks, not halt these exercises, which were filling NORAD's radar screens with false information? Myers's 'unavailability' is thus problematic in a way similar to that of Bush.

If we assume that the Islamic attackers had prepared their action long in advance, and that the public had only very limited knowledge of the exact date and times of the military exercises, one can wonder how such a fatal overlap could occur between attacks and military exercises.

9:00 According to the first official details released, Bush only now hears (from Andrew Card, his chief of staff, and others) about the attack on the World Trade Center: 12 minutes after many of Bush's staff and a global audience of millions had begun watching this tragedy unfold on TV.[1]

Initially it was assumed the President was just not informed, but later it turned out that various people had drawn his attention to the strike on the North Tower.[1,7]

9:00 Bush supposedly has a phone conversation with Condoleeza Rice;[1] according to Bush (three months after the attacks) in a response to an interview question from an 8-year-old child, he sees the strike on the North Tower on TV at around 9:01.[1]

Commentary: Since we are sure of the time that Andrew Card informed Bush of the second strike—9:04 or 9:05[1]—and since this information was given to him, in the video from Booker School, Sarasota,[2] after only about three minutes of the lesson held in his presence, both the conversation with Rice and Bush's account of seeing the attacks on TV are highly improbable due to time factors. (See article on p. 29f. Why did he not interrupt his visit to Booker School at this point?)[1]

9:00 (9:02, 9:03)—**around 9:25** (9:16) Bush attends a grade 2 class at Booker Elementary School. The class reads the story of a girl and her goat.[1]

Note: The President doesn't read out loud himself, but just listens to the class, then makes a few remarks in praise of the pupils and *waits* until the class is over.

During this time Bush is completely cut off, or you might say withdrawn, from the dramatic sequence of attacks, apart from Andrew Card's brief remarks to him (see under 9:05).[1]

Problem point: Bush does not regard it as necessary to interrupt his visit to the school to concern himself with the consequences of the attacks, or to respond to the danger implicit in the further missing aircraft, particularly given the (erroneous) assertion later made that only the President can give the order to shoot down an aeroplane.[1] Nor is any consideration given to evacuating the school which, due to its proximity to the airport, could have been the target of another unexpected attack.[2]

9:02:54 (according to seismographic recordings; according to other sources 9:03, 9:02)[1] aircraft WTC 2 (Flight 175) strikes the South Tower, between the 78th and 84th floor. The aeroplane strikes more or less the right corner of the façade,[4,8] which means:

- a large proportion of the plane's fuel burns up on the façade's exterior,[4,8]
- damage to the interior of the building (compared with the North Tower) is caused less by combustion heat than the force of the explosion,[4,8]
- a member of staff in the upper storeys (Brian Clark,

descending from the 84th floor) is able to descend via the centre stairs, passing the ruins of the aeroplane. At the 81st floor (!) he frees another employee (S. Praimnath) whose exit is blocked.[9]

Commentary: This dramatic rescue (and duration of stay) over several minutes is evidence that heat radiation was limited and that the steel supports[4,8] in the building's interior structure sustained only minor damage. Other supporting or structural elements included the steel framework and 13 cm-thick glass[10] of the façade, as well as the cross struts and steel sheets in the floor structure.[4,10] Despite the damage being slight in comparison with the North Tower, this building collapsed first.

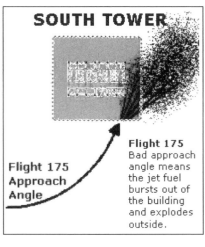
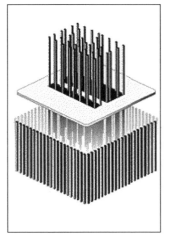

Strike on the South Tower[8]

The strike by aircraft WTC 2 (Flight UA 175) was also filmed by two amateur filmmakers. Gerhard Wisnewski's subsequent research has shown that the plane on one of these two recordings (by a camera team that by chance, from 8:43 onwards, was filming work on a gas pipe in immediate proximity to the twin towers) has a marked enlargement of the lower fuselage. This was demonstrably not the case with the aircraft of Flight UA 175 at the time it took off.[11,12]

Commentary: Since it clearly isn't possible to undertake such a structural alteration during a flight, some sources conclude that this is a different aircraft, and that the aircraft of UA 175 was swapped for another plane. These recordings showing the enlarged fuselage were also used by numerous media disseminating the US government's official view, but of course without reference to this detail.

The other amateur film does not show the plane but the South Tower immediately before WTC 2 struck.[13,19] Roughly four seconds before the strike, a winking light (about one to two storeys in size) appears at the left side of the façade, and moves diagonally downwards. Before arriving at the very righthand edge it vanishes, and fractions of a second later aircraft WTC 2 strikes just below the point where the light was last seen. This light appears shortly before WTC 2 undertakes its very adroit course correction and hits the South Tower, which it would otherwise have missed, by looping to the left.

Commentary: At first glance it may seem unfounded to link a point of light on the building with the aeroplane. However, in the war in Afghanistan, American soldiers at the front marked certain enemy locations with a laser beam so that target-seeking equipment could register them and aircraft could bomb them from the air. If the point of light on the façade is not just coincidence, it could be linked, firstly, with a 'target-marking instrument', and secondly with target-seeking equipment, as *technical* support for the strike by WTC 2 on the South Tower. Due to lack of technical facilities, the swapping of the aircraft necessary under such circumstances, and use of this light beam, could hardly be carried out by 'Islamic hijackers'. Certain circles within the American military or secret service, on the other hand, might well have access to such technical capacities. It is quite impossible that this flashing point of light on the façade was caused by the sun's reflection on part of the aeroplane. In this case the light would not flash as it did, quite apart from the fact that the sun would have had to shine from a different direction to have caused such an effect. The precise nature of this point of light has been examined by Henrik Melvang in his video, and his investigations on this are due to appear in book form.[13]

9:05 (9:06; 9:04 in the timeline issued by a website with links to the government[14]) Andrew Card approaches the President and whispers something into his ear. According to subsequent and to some extent divergent statements by Card and Bush, Card said: 'A second airplane has hit the World Trade Center' (Card), or 'America is under attack' (Bush). Ari Fleischer, who has since resigned as White House spokesman, showed Bush a sheet off-camera, on which was written: 'Don't say anything yet.' Without Bush issuing any instructions, and without Card expecting any, Card leaves the room, and Bush continues to observe the lesson.[1] The questionable motive, also cited by some media, was that Bush did not wish to disappoint or alarm the children who had so much looked forward to his visit.[1,7]

Further grounds given are that Bush initially thought it was an accident and did not want to act without reflection. He therefore waited for a full knowledge of the situation. If one considers the whole information service surrounding the head of state (besides secret servicemen and close colleagues, there was also a member of staff entrusted with receiving Bush's telephone messages and passing them on to him), Bush's statement that he initially thought there had been an

Two simultaneous pictures of 9:03[1]

accident appears wholly unbelievable.[1] (See also the commentary to 9:29.)

9:16 FAA (civil aviation control) informs NORAD that Flight 93 has probably been hijacked.[1]

9:20 (9:26, 9:49) All aeroplanes in American airports grounded.[1]

9:22 Some sources state that a fighter plane is seen in the vicinity of Flight 93.[1]

9:24 (9:25) NORAD is informed that Flight 77 (aircraft P) has probably been hijacked and is heading for Washington.[1]

9:27 According to Myers: NORAD orders two F-16 fighter planes from Langley military base to intercept Flight 77 (aircraft P). Distance between Langley and Washington: 129 miles; at a speed of 1,300 mph they would have been in Washington within 6 minutes. At 9:30 the two F-16s take off, and at the time aircraft P (Flight 77, supposedly) strikes the Pentagon, they are still said to be 105 miles away, which means they were travelling at a very slow speed for these fighter planes, of 120–130 mph.[1]

Commentary: Since it is unimaginable, particularly given the attacks on the two towers immediately prior to this, that fighter planes would fly at such slow speeds, this information seems less indicative of an emergency military intervention than of a 'botched' (poorly thought-out) retrospective fabrication in which the fighter planes allegedly arrived on the scene too late (see also 8:46, 9:41). This is also backed up by the fact that no one (NORAD? The secret services?) entrusted this important task to the St Andrews military base, which is only 10 miles distant from the Pentagon. It would no doubt have been impossible to claim that an aeroplane from this base had arrived too late.[15]

9:29 (9:16, 9:25; according to the first official announcements on CNN, possibly not until 9:30[7]) Bush leaves the classroom and speaks to journalists of an 'apparent terrorist attack on our country'.[1]

9:29 (9:16, 9:25) A (supposed) telephone conversation between Bush and security adviser Rice (may also not have taken place until after his TV appearance—see below), and discussions with colleagues.[1]

9:29 (9:30) A speech by Bush broadcast on TV with a minute's silence for the victims. Still no instructions issued in order to avert the danger (two aeroplanes that have left their flight path altogether).[1]

Commentary: From about the middle of 2003, some of the timelines show Bush's visit to the class as shortened to between 9:03 and 9:16, thus giving space for a full discussion between the President and his security forces, and combating the accusation of Bush's passivity. But in fact this 'correction' increases the power of such a reproach. Since the secret services had set up an open line to the ground stations from 8:40, Bush, after a full discussion and before entering the classroom, would have known not only about the first attack on the North Tower but probably also about the second attack on the South Tower (or at least that a second missing aeroplane had entered New York air space). Via the open line the secret service could also have known about Flight 77, missing since 8:56, and passed this information to Bush. Measures should have been taken to counter this immediate threat. After his school visit, the President, as the person with supreme responsibility, must have known about the probable hijacking of Flight 93 since 9:16, and (due to the delays in communication with NORAD) about missing Flight 77 (aircraft P). After the first attacks, two missing aeroplanes represented a further direct threat. Since, in the case of aeroplane hijackings, information is coordinated at the NMCC in the Pentagon, one should assume that this news could be passed directly to the top decision-makers to allow immediate measures to be taken in such a dire situation. The school visit, the discussions with the security forces without taking or ordering any specific measures, the statement to journalists and the subsequent TV appearance seem extraordinarily irresponsible and negligent against this background of time slipping away. Bush's conduct strikes one as generally deceitful, his facial expression on this film sequence and on photographs is unable to conceal a sense of guilt.[15]

9:30 (9:40) Transponder and radar contact with Flight 93 is lost.[1]

9:32 In an emergency measure, secret service agents take Vice-President Cheney from his office at the White House to the safety of an underground bunker.[1]

Commentary: Why are President Bush and the pupils (!) not taken to safety?

9:32 Per Stig Møller, who later became Denmark's foreign minister, and was in Washington at the time, stated: 'I saw smoke and fire rising up from the Pentagon at 9:32. My first impression was that a bomb had been detonated at the Pentagon.' (Denmark Radio P3, 12 September, 7.30 am.) Other witnesses also said they had the impression of an explosion.[13]

9:32 Flight P (Flight 77) makes a sudden turn over Washington, heading towards the Pentagon and falling very quickly from a height of 7,000 feet to ground level, thus descending below radar level.[1]

For 37 minutes this plane crossed American airspace unnoticed as it headed towards Washington. The Pentagon was not warned, the nearby St Andrews military airport entrusted with defence of the US capital (about ten miles away from the Pentagon, and where, at this time several squadrons of F-18 interceptor or fighter planes were stationed[2]) sent no planes (see commentary to 9:41).

9:36 (9:35) Aircraft S (Flight 93) turns towards Washington.[1]

9:41 (9:38–9:43, 9:45) Aircraft P (Flight 77) strikes (at ground level) into a part of the Pentagon that is being renovated.[1] There are no seismographic recordings of this aircraft strike.[1]

Commentary: The plane strikes the façade diagonally and penetrates three buildings lying one behind the other[16] (in other words, six exterior walls, which in this building are supposed to be of more solid than normal construction). Compared with the strike on the South Tower of the WTC this testifies to a more powerful penetrative force. However, this penetrative force is

 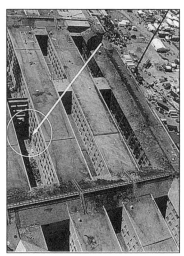

Exit hole of the flying object at the Pentagon[16]

confined to the fuselage area of the flying object. These aspects alone create doubt about the official announcements. Was this really Flight 77 or another type of flying object? The thorough investigations by Thierry Meyssan[16] and Eric Hufschmid[4] point clearly to some other flying object. Only some salient details are given here. The construction type of this wide-bodied aeroplane (in the Boeing 757 the height from the lower part of the turbine to the top surface of the fuselage measures 5.5 metres) would have meant two storeys were affected in such a strike. In order to impact on the ground floor only, the plane would have had to dig itself into the ground to a depth of between 1 and 2 metres.

Yet photographs show that the ground was left unscathed.[4] Neither obvious remnants of a wide-bodied aircraft nor passengers' bodies were found at the Pen-

American Airlines Flight 77, a Boeing 757[1]

tagon, although these bodies were indeed delivered to the mortuary some time later.[4] The size of the single turbine found at the site indicates a drone, which would also explain what would have been a highly complex manoeuvre for a wide-bodied aircraft by an inexperienced pilot at ground level.[4] The question is: what happened to Flight 77?

Grass left unscathed by the Boeing 757 (shown as outline)[4]

9:41 (later according to other sources) Bush reaches Sarasota airport and the presidential aircraft Airforce One.[1]

A few minutes after the strike on the Pentagon, interceptor planes take off from St Andrews military airport on the orders of the secret service, and give Washington protective cover.

Commentary: Why didn't they take off sooner? Why did the secret service not give the order before this, since, via the open line, they had known of all the flight movements since 8:40? Until 9:30 (in the official view) such an action would have halted the attack by aircraft P (Flight 77).

9:45 The White House is evacuated.[1]

9:48 The Capitol is evacuated.[1]

9:55 (9:57) Bush leaves Sarasota airport in his plane.[1]

9.55–11.55 Air Force One circles in American airspace, frequently changing direction. A direct flight to Washington seems unsafe since the plane is flying unaccompanied. One has to ask why military aircraft cannot accompany Air Force One and guarantee it safety.[1]

Commentary: During this flight Bush, or one of the members of his staff, first compares the attacks with the apparently surprise attack by the Japanese on Pearl Harbor (7 December 1941). This comparison, later reiterated several times by various leading figures (e.g. Zbigniew Brzezinski) aims to kindle the American people's patriotic feelings. The analogy deserves serious attention since Washington knew in advance about the provoked Japanese attack, and did not warn those in charge at the Pearl Harbor base. After this supposedly surprise attack, Roosevelt won the support of Congress and the American people for bringing the USA into the Second World War.[17]

9:59:04 (according to seismographic recordings) The South Tower collapses uniformly into itself[1] (56 minutes after the strike) in a way that otherwise only occurs in a 'controlled demolition'.

Commentary: Since the building's support structure was only damaged at one corner, a sideways collapse of the upper portion (due to excess stress on the support structure from the weight of the upper storeys) would have been more likely. It is also surprising that the South Tower was the first to collapse, despite sustaining less damage from the strike and having been hit 17 minutes later. This indicates the use of explosives inside the building.[4,13] (See also 10:28:31.)

10:06 Aircraft S (Flight 93) crashes near Shanksville. There are faint seismographic recordings of this crash. The aircraft is completely destroyed. Part of the engine weighing half a tonne is found over a mile away from the crash site. Various eyewitnesses report having seen a military aircraft in the immediate vicinity.[1]

Other witness statements and Gerhard Wisnewski's enquiries seem to contradict reports of the crash of a wide-bodied aircraft. At the supposed crash site there was only undefinable scrap and equally undefinable body parts, which, additionally, showed no signs of blood. Forensic medicine was unable to calculate the precise time of death. Some sources suggest therefore that these may have been old corpse parts.[11]

Commentary: The facts relating to this crash suggest also that the original UA 93 aircraft may have been swapped for a different flying object.

10:10 (15) The part of the Pentagon that was hit collapses.

10:28:31 (according to seismographic recordings) The North Tower collapses, also uniformly into itself, one hour and twenty minutes after being hit.[1]

When the World Trade Center collapsed, witnesses spoke of hearing a swift succession of explosions,[13] see also Eric Hufschmid.[4]

Commentary: Five days after the collapse of the towers, and despite spraying with cold water, the surface of rubble in many places was still as hot as 500° to 700° celsius. These temperatures, and damage to the very solid steel supports in the tower, cannot be ascribed to the fire, but rather to explosions caused by a 'controlled demolition'.[4] The facts clearly suggest the use of explosive.

15:00 Very locally restricted fire in building 7 (7th and 12th storeys).[4]

Between **16:00** and **17:00** Photographer Tom Franklin states that fire fighters evacuated the area and hoisted a flag.[4]

17:25 Collapse of building 7, although only small fires were burning. In contrast to the collapse of the North and South Towers and building 7, buildings 5 and 6 did not collapse despite burning very vigorously. According to research by Eric Hufschmid, the area between the 23rd and 25th storey of building 7 had been converted into a reinforced bunker. This possessed explosion-resistant windows and walls, its own air and water supplies, and three emergency power units. It was capable of resisting both biological and bomb attacks. Hufschmid states that this was the command centre for the computer-controlled destruction of the World Trade Center, and that from this vantage point the whole occurrence could be observed without danger. Subsequently building 7, and the evidence, had to be removed.[4]

There is a striking quote by Larry Silverstein relating to the controlled demolition of building 7: 'I remember getting a call from the fire department commander, telling me that they were not sure they were gonna be able to contain the fire, and I said, "We've had such terrible loss of life, maybe the smartest thing to do is pull it." And they made that decision to pull and we watched the building collapse.'[18]

Commentary: Why couldn't these small fires be contained? One has to wonder whether the other buildings also collapsed in a controlled demolition.

19:00 (approximately) Bush and Powell (the latter returns from Lima, Peru) reach the White House.[1]

20:30 Bush addresses the American nation in a TV broadcast.[1]

José García Morales

Notes

Notes to Introduction

1. *Mythos 9/11, Der Warheit auf der Spur* ('The myth of 9/11, Tracking down the truth'), Droemer/Knaur, Munich 2004.
2. The number of Pearl Harbor victims was 2,476, while recent estimates of those in New York are under 3,000.
3. This can be found at http://www.9-11commission.gov. The passage by Roberta Wohlstetter cited in the report is taken from there.
4. From: http://www.9-11commission.gov/hearings/index.htm.
5. See note 3 above.
6. See note 3 above.
7. BBC World Service 22 July, 2004 (author's emphasis).
8. A transcript of this interview can be found at http://www.9-11comission.gov/hearings/index.htm. For a while it was possible to order it as a video under ISBN number 0-7806-4006-3 from the PBS website, until the PBS shop stopped supplying it. (At http://youthfulindiscretions.com, a picture version can be downloaded, and at http://Vestigial Conscience.com/PullIt.mp3, a recording of the soundtrack.)

    Representatives of the victims' relatives urged New York Mayor Giuliani to debate Silverstein's comment with the official investigative commission (http:www.911independentcommission.org/giulia

ni31804.html). Silverstein's key statement is not mentioned anywhere in the commission's concluding report.

9. For further comprehensive views of an *occult-political nature*, see the introduction to the simultaneously published text *Brückenbauer müssen die Menschen werden* ('Human beings must become bridge builders'), ed. Thomas Meyer, Perseus Verlag 2004.

10. Overcoming the contrast between percept and concept is achieved through the act of knowledge. This reveals the higher unity which is hidden in both. In R. Steiner's fundamental philosophical work *Truth and Science*, knowledge is defined as a *synthesis* of perception and concept. It is distinguished both from perception without thought and from abstract constructions which have largely lost their connection with perception. Among other things the latter characteristically embody all legends or 'myths' such as the official myth of September 11.

11. *Mythos 9/11, Der Wahrheit auf der Spur*, Munich 2004, p. 251f.

12. R. Steiner *Gegenwärtiges und Vargangenes im Menschengeiste*, GA 167, Rudolf Steiner Verlag.

13. See for example Steiner's lectures on *Faust* (*Das Faust-Problem*), dated 3 and 4 November 1917, GA 273, Rudolf Steiner Verlag.

14. See note 12 above.

Notes in Chapter 1
(This article first appeared in the *Basler Zeitung* on 4.11.2002.)

1. http://www.cryan.com/war/speech

2. *The Clash of Civilizations and the Remaking of World Order*, Simon & Schuster, New York 1996.

3. Z. Brzezinski, *The Grand Chessboard, American Primacy and its Geostrategic Imperatives*, New York 1997, p. 211 (also chapter 6).

4. Interview in the *Europäer*, July-August 2002. Cf. also von Bülow's book *Im Namen des Staates*, Munich (Piper series) 2000.

5. http://www.whitehouse.gov/news/releases/2001/09/20010926-3.html. See also the picture on page 57.

6. *Times of India*, 9 October 2001. A detailed account of the links between the ISI and CIA can be found in: Michael Chossudovsky, *War and Globalization, the Truth Behind September 11*, Shanty Bay (Canada), 2002, chapters 4 and 10.

Notes in Chapter 2

1. CNN Live Event/Special, 12.59, Jan. 2002: 'Bush speaks at Town hall meeting' by Jonathan Karl.

2. 'The President as Incompetent Liar': www.emperors-clothes.com/indict/liar.htm.

Notes in Chapter 3

1. 'Truth is great and will be victorious': motto in the book *FDR, The Other Side Of The Coin, How We Were Tricked Into World War II*, by Hamilton Fish. Fish was the son of a member of Congress, the grandson of a Governor of New York and Foreign Minister, and the great grandson of a lieutenant in Washington's army and friend of Lafayette. He graduated in political science and history from Harvard, and from 1945 served as Republican

member of Congress. Fish's date of birth is 7 December, date of the later attack on Pearl Harbor.

2. *Time* magazine, September 11, 2001.
3. Documented in Schweizer Fernsehen, September 2001, author's archive. Chief of Staff Card, who whispered the dire news into Bush's ear, was also on board this flight.
4. See the first part of this article in the October issue of the *Europäer*.
5. *Le Temps*, 13 September 2001.
6. *Day of Deceit, The Truth About FDR and Pearl Harbor*, Simon & Schuster, Touchstone, New York 2001.
7. *Pearl Harbor 1941, eine amerikanische Katastrophe*, Herbig 2000 (3rd edition).
8. Yet another witness for the prosecution in relation to Pearl Harbor is Admiral Kimmel, the fleet commander at Hawaii, from whom was withheld all decisive information prior to 7 December 1941. His book, *Admiral Kimmel's Story*, was published in 1955 in New York. Karlheinz Deschner also discusses a true version of the Pearl Harbor events in his book *Der Moloch, Zur Amerikanisierung der Welt*, Stuttgart 1992, p. 259ff.
9. R. Steiner: *Zeitgeschichtliche Betrachtungen*, vol. 1, GA 173, Rudolf Steiner Verlag. English edition: *The Karma of Untruthfulness, Vol 1.*, Rudolf Steiner Press, London 1988.
10. If, in this case, certain circles had taken on the task of exploiting the terrorist potential, of monitoring preparations for the suicide and ensuring, through a covert operation, that these were not impeded, then the comparison with Pearl Harbor would largely be exact.

In a German TV discussion (Club, SF2, 13 October

2001) Andreas von Bülow, member of the German parliament, secretary of state and federal minister for research and technology until 1982, voiced the suspicion that the work of the well-informed FBI must have been 'neutralized' by the CIA at some point. Bülow is the author of a book entitled *Im Namen des Staates, CIA, BND und die kriminellen Machenschaften der Geheimdienste*, ('On behalf of the state, CIA, BND and the criminal machinations of the secret services'), Munich 2000.

11. www.whitehouse.gov/news/releases/2001/09/20010926-3.html. See also the picture on p. 57.

12. In July 1990 the American ambassador April Glaspie, on behalf of James Baker, misled Iraq into thinking that the USA regarded Iraq's invasion of Kuwait was an internal Iraqi affair. Following the invasion the USA stage-managed a huge propaganda story to enlist public opinion in favour of an American intervention. Cf. Deschner, op. cit., p. 368ff.

13. Rudolf Steiner on 22 March 1909, *Geisteswissenschaftliche Menschenkunde*, Rudolf Steiner Verlag, GA 107.

Notes in Chapter 4

This article appeared in the *Basler Zeitung* on 17 October 2003. A fuller version appeared in the *Europäer*, year 7, issue 12, p. 8ff. (See archive at www.perseus.ch)

1. Bob Woodward: *Bush at War*, Simon & Schuster 2002.

2. *Time* magazine, September 11, 2001.

3. Cf. for instance Anthony Sutton, *Wall Street and the Rise of Hitler*, Suffolk 1976.

4. Detailed references in: *Der Europäer*, year 7, issue 12.
5. Richard Bernstein, *The New York Times* Book Review. Source: http://www.pearlharbor41.com/praise.htm.
6. Woodward, op. cit., p. 38.
7. Public hearing 31.3.2003. See: www.9-11commission.gov/
8. 'January 16, 1997: Albert Wohlstetter, R.I.P'. at www.polyconomics.com/searchbase/fyi01-16-97.html.

Notes in Chapter 5
(This article first appeared in the *Basler Zeitung* on 9 April 2003.)
1. On 21 August 1920, *Geisteswissenschaft als Erkenntnis der Grundimpulse sozialer Gestaltung* (Rudolf Steiner Verlag, GA 199).
2. Nafeez M. Ahmed, *The War on Freedom, How and Why America was Attacked, September 11, 2001*, Tree of Life Publications, 2002. New expanded edition: *The War on Truth, Disinformation and the Anatomy of Terrorism*, Arris Books 2005.
3. Gore Vidal: *Dreaming War, Blood for Oil and the Cheney-Bush Junta*, Clairview Books, Sussex 2003.
4. Barry Zwicker, in: *September 2001, Coverup or Complicity*, at www.global-research.ca.
5. *GEO* magazine, Hamburg, May 2001, p. 89.
6. *Foreign Relations of the United States*, 1948, Volume I, pp. 509–529.

Notes in Chapter 6
(This article first appeared in the *Europäer*, year 7, issue 2/3, December–January 2002/03.)

1. Cf. Michael C. Ruppert: '*11/20/01—THE "F" WORD—the Patriot Act: What "Imperial" decisions by Bush and Ashcroft have done to your Civil Liberties since 9-11.*' Ruppert has since published his bestselling book: *Crossing the Rubicon, The Decline of the American Empire at the End of the Age of Oil*, New Society Publishers, Gabriola Island 2004.

2. On 9 November 1918 Wilhelm II abdicated as emperor; 9 November 1923: Hitler's attempted but failed coup; 9 November 1938: 'Kristallnacht': the burning of Jewish shops and synagogues in Berlin and throughout Germany; 9 November 1989: the fall of the Berlin Wall.

3. Zbigniew Brzezinski, *The Grand Chessboard, American Primacy and its Geostrategic Imperatives*, New York 1997, p. 211.

4. On 30 July 1918, Steiner stated that 'radical evil' would come from America (*Erdensterben und Weltenleben, Anthroposophische Lebensgaben*, Rudolf Steiner Verlag, GA 181). At the beginning of November 1919 he refers to the incarnation of Ahriman in the West, 'before the third millennium has properly begun' (*Der innere Aspekt des sozialen Rätsels*, Rudolf Steiner Verlag, GA 193. English edition: *The Ahrimanic Deception*, Anthroposophic Press, New York 1985). 'Ahriman' is the name given in spiritual science to an entity or being which promotes materialism and materialistic intellectualism. The evil that manifested in Nazism and the 'gulag' system may in the distant future appear as the prelude to the onset of this radical evil. Cooperation with Nazism before, during and after the Second World War by American financial and banking circles (which included the grandfather of the

current President, Prescott Bush) is something Ruppert also refers to.

In connection with this complex of issues—which has not yet been thoroughly investigated—I would like to mention the following works: A. Sutton, *Wall Street and the Rise of Hitler*, Bloomfield Books, Sudbury 1976; and Webster G. Tarpley and Anton Chaitkin, *George Bush, The Unauthorized Biography*, Executive Intelligence Review, 1991. This latter, thoroughly researched, work not only highlights the involvement of Prescott Bush in business conducted with Nazi Germany, but also American interest in German eugenics research. Prescott Bush was, like the current President and his father, a member of the Yale Skull & Bones club. In the latest publication about this club by Alexandra Robbins (*Secrets of the Tomb*, Boston, New York, London 2002), the very real connection between Prescott Bush and Nazi Germany is, however, played down. Finally, there is the book by Christopher Simpson: *Blowback, America's Recruitment of Nazis and Its Effects on the Cold War*, London 1988.

Notes in Chapter 7

(This article first appeared in *Der Europäer*, year 4, issue 12, October 2000.)

1. Steiner drew attention to the links between Anglo-American politics and Hegel's philosophy on 4 December 1920 (*Die Brücke zwischen der Weltgeistigkeit und dem Physischen des Menschen*, Rudolf Steiner Verlag, GA 202; cf. also *Der Europäer*, Vol. 4, issue 11, p. 14). We are grateful to Anthony Sutton (1925–2002), who was very probably unaware of this important suggestion by

Steiner, for having verified it *de facto* in his investigations of the Skull & Bones fraternity.

2. Hegel, *Wissenschaft der Logik*, part I, note 3. Suhrkamp Werkausgabe, vol. 5, p. 100.

3. 'The bud vanishes as the blossom breaks forth, and one could say that the one is refuted by the other. Likewise the blossom is declared erroneous in its existence by the fruit, as the latter's reality replaces that of the former. These forms are not only distinct from each other, but also suppress one another as mutually incompatible. However, their fluid nature at the same time renders them moments of organic unity in which they not only conflict with each other but are each as necessary as the other, and this same necessity alone is what makes the life of the whole possible.' Hegel, *Phänomenologie des Geistes*, Preface.

4. Rudolf Steiner's ideas about money represent the only approach which nowadays takes account of both developmental moments by including money's devaluation as an intrinsic part of its creation, thus lending money a value which is of limited duration.

5. One can study this in relation to the negotiations which the USA leads between Israel and Palestine, China and Taiwan, and Serbia, Bosnia, Kosovo etc.

6. In this regard, the most important result of NATO's war against Serbia is the now more or less permanent local US presence in the Balkans. This is apparent, for instance, in the creation of new military bases, or in the increased dependency of the region on western financial aid.

7. The old phrase 'divide and rule' illustrates such a strategy. An excellent recent example of apparent but

false negotiations, which in fact gave rise to a pretext for war, were the Rambouillet negotiations, following whose programmed collapse NATO initiated its attacks on Serbia. The decisive factor which unleashed the much-lamented 'humanitarian catastrophe'—to avert which this war was supposedly fought—can be found in the insincere nature of such negotiations.

8. Cf. Andreas Bracher: *Regine Igel, Andreotti. Politik zwischen Geheimdienst und Mafia*, in *Der Europäer*, year 2, issue 7, p. 17.

9. In *Philosophy and Anthroposophy*, Mercury Press, Spring Valley 1988 (GA 35).

10. *Briefe Band II: 1890–1925*, Rudolf Steiner Verlag, (GA 39) p. 227.

11. In chapter 4 of *Intuitive Thinking as a Spiritual Path* (Anthroposophic Press 1995), Steiner says: 'Therefore what I have said about the nature of thinking—that it rests within itself and is determined by nothing—cannot simply be transferred to concepts. (I note this explicitly here, because this is where I differ from Hegel, who posits the concept as first and original.)'

12. See chapter 6, note 4.

13. 'Das Ewige in der Hegelschen Logik und ihr Gegenbild im Marxismus', lecture of 27 August 1920, on the 150th anniversary of Hegel's birth. Published in *Geisteswissenschaft als Erkenntnis der Grundimpulse sozialer Gestaltung*, Rudolf Steiner Verlag (GA 199).

14. 'Preserved' here has the dual Hegelian meaning of being both something finished and yet also, simultaneously, continuing to exist as a yeast or ferment in the new, thus ensuring the *continuity* of evolution.

15. GA 266/1, p.49f. Further comments by Steiner on *Light on the Path* can be found in *Guidance in Esoteric Training*, Rudolf Steiner Press, London 2001 (GA 268), in particular the chapter there entitled 'Exegesis to *Light on the Path*'.

Notes in Chapter 8

1. Lecture of 6 November 1917, GA 178. English translation: *Secret Brotherhoods and the Mystery of the Human Double* (Rudolf Steiner Press, Sussex 2004).
2. This was not the case in former times. In ancient times the 'most spiritual' person was also the most powerful, as the old priest-king tradition demonstrates. Rudolf Steiner said that the last 'initiate' (or spiritually highly developed person) to hold a position as ruler was Charles IV, the Rosicrucian and architect of Karlstein Castle near Prague.

Notes to Timeline for 9.11.2001

1. http://cooperativeresearch/org/completetimeline/ 'Part 3: Day of 9-11, minute-by-minute'. Details on Bush can also be found at Paul Thompson's website, see 'Day of 911' at http://www.cooperativeresearch.org/project.jsp?project=911_project.
2. http://emperors-clothes.com/indict/indict-1.htm and http://emperors-clothes.com/indict/indict-3.htm.
3. Wolfgang Effenberger, Konrad Löw: *Pax americana, Die Geschichte einer Weltmacht von ihren angelsächsischen Wurzeln bis heute*, Herbig Verlag, Munich 2004, p. 381.
4. Eric Hufschmid, *Painful Questions, An Analysis of the*

September 11 Attack, Goleta (CA) 2002. His video can be downloaded at http://question911.com/index.htm.

5. http://www.cooperativeresearch.org/timeline.jsp? timeline = complete_911_timeline&theme = coverup&startpos = 100.

6. Michael Ruppert: *Crossing the Rubicon, The Decline of the American Empire at the End of the Age of Oil* (New Society Publishers, Gabriola Island 2004) chapters 18–21.

7. http://www.communitycurrency.org/Main IndexMX.html.

8. http://www.serendipity.li/wtc.htm and http://www.serendipity.li/wtc2.htm.

9. Stefan Aust, Cordt Schnibben (eds.), *11. September, Geschichte eines Terrorangriffs*, Spiegel Buchverlag, Hamburg 2002.

10. Andreas von Bülow, *Die CIA und der 11. September, Internationaler Terror und die Rolle der Geheimdienste.* Munich, Zurich 2003.

11. Gerhard Wisnewski, *Mythos 9/11, Der Wahrheit auf der Spur.* Knaur, Munich 2004.

12. www.rense.com/general14/boeing.htm. Further information about the anomalies of UA 175 can be found at: http://www.911inplanesite.com/ and http://www.amics21.com/911/flight175/.

13. www.bombsinsidewtc.dk. Video by Henrick Malvang: *Bomberne som forsvandt.*

14. http://www.september11news.com/PresidentBush.html.

15. http://www.medienanalyse-international.de/ueber-blick.html features photos of Bush at Sarasota after receiving the news from Andrew Card and a timeline for 9/11 including '3 seconds'.

16. Thierry Meyssan, Pentagate, Carnot Publishing Ltd., London 2002.
17. Cf. also the articles by T. Meyer on p. 37 and p. 65. Also George Morgenstern, *Pearl Harbor, The Story of the Secret War*, Devin Adair Company, New York 1947.
18. http://www.911citizenswatch.org/print.php?sid=422.
19. http://www.CameraPlanet.com/7days/. Video: '7 days in September', scene with Lightpoint, by Jennifer Spell.

Index